FREE TO BE... YOU AND ME

and

FREE TO BE... A FAMILY

Free to Be . . . You and Me

AND

Free to Be . . . A Family

Created by Marlo Thomas

Developed and Edited by
Christopher Cerf, Carole Hart,
Francine Klagsburn,
Letty Cottin Pogrebin, Mary Rodgers,
and Marlo Thomas

Designed by Samuel N. Antupit
and Barbara Cohen

RUNNING PRESS
PHILADELPHIA · LONDON

Contributing Editors: Carol Hall, Sarah Durkee, Wendy Goldwyn Batteau, and Norman Stiles
Running Press Editor: Patricia Aitken Smith
Musical Arrangements by Stephen Lawrence and Paul Jacobs

Advisors

James P. Comer, M.D., Maurice Falk Professor of Child Psychiatry, Yale University Child Study Center

Maureen Crossmaker, Project Director for Assault Prevention Training, National Assault Prevention Center

Merle Froschl, Founder and Co-Coordinator, Women and Disability Awareness Project,
and Co-Director, Educational Equity Concepts, Inc.

Ellen Galinsky, Director of Work and Family Life Studies, Bank Street College of Education

Margaret Gates, National Executive Director, Girls Clubs of America

Phyllis Katz, Ph. D., Director, Institute for Research on Social Problems

James Levine, Director, The Fatherhood Project, Bank Street College of Education

Joseph Pleck, Ph. D., Henry R. Luce Professor of Families, Change and Society, Wheaton College

Copyright © 1997, 1987, 1974 by the Free to Be Foundation, Inc.
All rights reserved under the Pan-American and International Copyright Conventions
Printed in the United States

9 8 7 6 5 4 3 2
Digit on the right indicates the number of this printing

Library of Congress Cataloging-in-Publication Number 97-076516

ISBN 0-7624-0327-6 paper
ISBN 0-7624-0328-4 hardcover

This book may be ordered by mail from the publisher.
Please include $2.50 for postage and handling. *But try your bookstore first!*

Running Press Book Publishers
125 South Twenty-second Street
Philadelphia, Pennsylvania 19103-4399

Special Thanks

To Eddie Adams, David Allender, Stuart Applebaum, Joanne Barkan, Karen Barnes, Karin Berg, Kathie Berlin, Marc Black, Dawn Bridges, David Britt, Sue Brownlees, Patricia T. Carbine, Seymour Chwast, Judie Clarke, Sally Cooper, Jean Enderson, Phyllis Flood, Michael Frith, Nancy Gallt, Angelina Genduso, Darcy Gilpin, Jay Harnick, Andrew Helfer, Jim Henson, Rudy Jordan, Jenette Kahn, Lisa Kennedy, Fern Khan, John Knapp, Danica Kombol, W. A. Krueger Co., Gary Lapow, Sharon Lerner, Robert F. Levine, Paul Levitz, Vinnie Liguori, Marilu Lopez, Sonia Manzano, Barry Marx, Maxwell Photographics, Inc., Dr. David Milrod, Kathryn Mullen, Manuel and Kate Neri, Mary Phylis, Jim Plumeri, Ann Poe, Jill Rabon, Nancy Rose, Lili Rosenstreich, Stephen Rubin, Richard Ruopp, Donna Ruvituso, Heidi Sachner, Lucy Salvino, Ray Sander, Nancy Sans, Herb Sargent, Kathryn Schenker, Jeff Segal, Virginia Solotaroff, Judy Stagnitto, Katie Swanson, Tani Takagi, Iwao Takamoto, Eric Taylor, Lily Tomlin, Rusty Unger, Jerry White, Vernon White, Marie Wilson, Perla Winer, Harriet Yassky, Jaye Zimet, to the Children, Parents, Teachers, and Staff of P.S. 146 in Manhattan and the Bank Street School and especially to Elizabeth Perle McKenna.

Grateful acknowledgment is made for permission to publish the following:

Words and music for "Free to Be . . . You and Me," "When We Grow Up," "Sisters and Brothers," and "Helping," copyright © 1972 Ms. Foundation for Women, Inc. Used by permission.

Words and music for "Parents Are People," "It's All Right To Cry," and "Glad To Have a Friend Like You" and words for "Housework" and "My Dog Is a Plumber," copyright © 1972 Free to Be Foundation, Inc.

"Atalanta," copyright © 1973 Free to Be Foundation, Inc.

"The Pain and the Great One" by Judy Blume. Original © 1974 Free to Be Foundation. Copyright assigned to Judy Blume March 19, 1984.

"The Southpaw" by Judith Viorst. Original © 1974 Free to Be Foundation. Copyright assigned to Judith Viorst January 1, 1994.

"Three Wishes" by Lucille Clifton. Copyright 1974 by Lucille Clifton. Used by permission of Delacorte Press, a division of Bantam Doublday Dell Publishing Group, Inc.

"William's Doll," adapted from the book *William's Doll* by Charlotte Zolotow. Text copyright © 1972 Charlotte Zolotow. Used by permission of HarperCollins Publishers. Words and music adaptation, copyright © 1972 Ms. Foundation for Women, Inc.

"Dudley Pippin and the Principal," by Phil Ressner, adapted from "Dudley and the Principal" from the book Dudley Pippin by Phil Ressner, illustrated by Arnold Lobel. Text copyright © 1965 Phil Ressner. Pictures copyright © 1965 Arnold Lobel. Reprinted by permission of HarperCollins, Publishers.

Photographs for "Parents Are People" and "It's All Right To Cry" from United Press International.

"A Father Like That," text copyright © 1971 by Charlotte Zolotow. Reprinted by permission of HarperCollins Publishers, Inc.

"I'll Fix Anthony," Text copyright © 1969 by Judith Viorst. Illustrations copyright 1969 by Arnold Lobel. Reprinted by permission of HarperCollins Publishers, Inc.

"Stevie," Copyright © 1969 by John L. Steptoe. Reprinted by permission of HarperCollins Publishers, Inc.

"Crowded Tub" and "The Little Boy and the Old Man," Copyright © 1981 by Evil Eye Music, Inc.

"And Superboy Makes 3," SUPERBOY, SUPERMAN and all other characters in "And Superboy Makes 3," their distinctive likenesses and related indicia, are trademarks of DC Comics Inc. Copyright © 1987 by DC Comics, Inc. Published under license.

"Somethings Don't Make Any Sense at All," Text copyright © 1981 by Judith Viorst. Reprinted by permission of Antheneum Publishers, Inc.

"On My Pond," Text copyright © 1987 by Splotched Animal Music and Jive Durkee Music. KERMIT THE FROG is a trademark of Henson Associates Inc. Illustrations copyright © 1987 by Henson Associates, Inc. "On My Pond" is adapted from a SESAME STREET sequence. SESAME STREET is a trademark and a service mark of Children's Television Workshop.

"Lily Tomlin's Edith Ann in And That's the Truth" copyright © 1987 by Lily Tomlin and Jane Wagner.

"All Us Come Cross the Water" Text copyright by © 1973 by Lucille Clifton. Illustrations copyright © 1973 by John L. Steptoe. "All Us Come Cross the Water" has been adapted for use in this publication. Originally published by Holt, Rinehart and Winston.

"Little Abigail and the Beautiful Pony," Copyright © 1981 by Evil Eye Music, Inc.

"Like Me," by Emily Kingsley was suggested by JUST LIKE ME, a book by Jennifer Fink.

Photos for The Fat Boys collage courtesy of Eddie Adams, Steve Friedman, Paul Natkin and Tin Pan Apple.

Photo for "Twanna and Me," copyright © 1987 by Jonathan Becker.

"Boy Meets Girl Plus One" by Peter Stone is based upon "Boy Meets Girl" by Peter Stone and Carl Reiner.

Musical arrangements for "Free to Be . . . A Family," "Friendly Neighborhood," "Jimmy Says," "It's Not My Fault," "In My Room," "I'm Never Afraid," "The Stupid Song," "Talk It Over," "The Biggest Problem (Is in Other People's Minds)," "On My Pond," "Something for Everyone," "Thank Someone," and "The Turn of the Tide."

Piano arrangements for *Free to Be . . . You and Me, When We Grow Up, Parents Are People, It's All Right to Cry, Glad to Have a Friend Like You, Sisters and Brothers, William's Doll,* and *Helping* by Stephen Lawrence.

Contents

Foreword

This book started very small, about three feet tall—the height of my niece Dionne when she asked me to read her a bedtime story—more than twenty-five years ago. It amazed me that most of the books I found for her back then were just that, books designed to put Dionne and her mind to sleep. They told stories of the good girl she ought to be—stories of the impossible girl that no girl ever was—but seldom stories of who she could really be if she felt free enough to imagine . . . everything.

I wanted a different kind of book for Dionne, one that would wake her up to her possibilities, a party of a book to celebrate who she was and all she could become. Many of my writer, poet and composer friends wanted the same for the children they loved—and these wonderfully talented and generous people donated their work to the project we called *Free to Be . . . You and Me*—a special new collection of stories, poems and songs that would help girls and boys feel free to be who they are and who they want to be.

As Dionne grew up and learned how BIG her life could be, I realized what children like her needed now was a really GIGANTIC book, roomy enough to contain all the things they had to know about the huge variety of people who cluster together and call themselves "family." The idea was that if you studied up on the folks in your family, chances are you would soon be an expert on how to get along in the big wide world when you grew up. *Free to Be . . . A Family* looked like a regular-sized book, but deep down inside, it was enormous. There was room in it for all the kinds of families that shelter and nuture children, all the kinds of friends and relations we are to each other, all the different kinds of households we live in and love in.

Free to Be . . . You and Me and *Free to Be . . . A Family* are like balloons. The more you read them and use them, the more they stretch, the bigger they become, and the more of the world you can see inside them. A lot of kids who are now grown-ups looked back on how their world stretched and grew while they read *Free to Be . . . You and Me* and *Free to Be . . . A Family* and they wanted the same big balloon experience for the children they love. So now we've taken stories, songs and poems from both books and created a SUPER GIGANTIC fun-filled *Free to Be* collection especially for you.

Each story changes with the voice that tells it; each picture is transformed by the eyes that see it. So go ahead, put your own personal stamp on this book. Write your name in big letters on the front. Read it aloud. Act it out. Sing it for all to hear.

Remember, this is a new party of a book. It's being thrown not just by those of us who wrote it, but by those who once read it, the children the grown-ups who love you used to be.

The party is being held in the country called "Us," in the town called "Possibilities," on the street called "Freedom"—to be, to become, to imagine . . . everything! The time is now. And you are all invited.

—*Marlo Thomas*

A Note to Parents, Teachers and Other Grown-up Friends

You are about to share an extraordinary experience with the children in your life.

Free to Be . . . You and Me is multi-layered entertainment—an adventure book because it opens new worlds, a humor book (but the laugh is on old stereotypes), a song and story book, a poetry collection, a picture gallery and more—all of it dedicated to the sense of wonder and curiosity that makes childhood a rich time of discovery, change, and growth.

For all its variety, this book is not just a happy hodge-podge; there is method to our merriment. Some of the selections are intended to expand children's horizons so that they can dream bigger dreams and invent their own futures. Other selections are meant to dispel some of the myths that hamper and hurt—like pretty-equals-good, big-boys-don't-cry, and all-mommies-belong-in-the-kitchen. Still others revisit the fairy tale tradition—only this time, Sleeping Beauty stays awake and the prince doesn't have to keep proving his "manhood."

Parents and friends of children are always searching for bedtime stories that we can read to kids that will help stimulate their growth and development. We want excitement without violence, fantasy without demeaning role-playing, stories that are accessible without being condescending, and art that illuminates without typecasting. We want human diversity, a celebration of life's bountiful choices, a literature that honors the mind, heart, and spirit of every child.

In fact, these are the very goals and values that fueled the first-rate writers and artists who have contributed to this book. Perhaps that is why love and vitality shine from every page. It's also why this book is both a fun and yet feisty rebuttal to those cultural influences that would stunt children's development by confining them to prisons of gender.

In *Free to Be . . . You and Me*, no game, toy, sport, job, idea, or aspiration is off limits to anyone. In this book, girls and boys can find their best selves and the best parts of each other.

If *Free to Be . . . You and Me* is about children's individuality, autonomy, and personal development, *Free to Be . . . A Family* is about togetherness and belonging, about Self and Other, about finding a balance between independence and attachment.

Some people believe that there is only one kind of family and only one way of living together. But kids know otherwise. In the United States, some adults and children live in "traditional" families (a small percentage of homes contain a stay-home mother, employed father, and their own biological children), while others live in stepfamilies, blended families, extended, adoptive, single parent, two-paycheck, or foster families, and still other household types have no name at all. We believe that, labelled or not, each family is the right kind of family if it knows how to nourish, nurture, and love its children.

Since a child's family is as vital to her or his core identity as gender, race, religion, or culture, it makes sense that the selections from *Free to Be . . . A Family* challenge family stereotypes in the same way that the selections from *Free to Be . . . You and Me* challenge sex and race stereotypes. We combined highlights from both books so that you can explore all of these important themes while delighting in the marvels of make-believe.

If you stop to think about it, you'll be able to decode the educational intent behind each story whether it's the message that brotherhood includes sisterhood, or the notion that cooperation is intrinsic to friendship, or the idea that one cannot achieve personal dignity without respecting others.

But if you don't stop to think about it, what you'll find here is pure enchantment—entertainment that will bring joy into your home or classroom and light up your children's lives. So grab a guitar, sit down at the piano, or snuggle with someone at bedtime and start enjoying this book. There's something in it for the free spirit in every grown-up and the wise soul in every child.

—Letty Cottin Pogrebin

What Buying This Book Will Do

The book you are holding in your hands right now is unique in many ways. Most of them you will see by reading and looking, but one of the most important differences can't be seen at all. That is where the money is going.

The proud creators of this book—along with the writers and artists and poets and musicians and all those many people who worked long and lovingly to put it together—care about its message so much that they decided not to take their usual royalties from any profits that might result. Instead, that past and future money has been and will continue to be contributed to the Free to Be Foundation. There, it is distributed to multi-racial projects all over the country: projects that protect children from danger and help them stay with people who love and care for them; that make sure children's unique talents aren't limited because of race, gender, poverty, or other unfairness; and, that help children stay healthy and grow up free.

This project was born of love and hope. Thanks for your support, it will also make love and hope tangible.

—*Gloria Steinem*

FREE TO BE... YOU AND ME

and

FREE TO BE... A FAMILY

Free to Be...You and Me

♪ music on page 210

There's a land that I see
Where the children are free.
And I say it ain't far
To this land, from where we are.

Take my hand. Come with me,
Where the children are free.
Come with me, take my hand,
And we'll live . . .

I see a land, bright and clear,
And the time's coming near,
When we'll live in this land,
You and me, hand-in-hand.

Take my hand. Come along,
Lend your voice to my song.
Come along. Take my hand,
Sing a song . . .

In a land
Where the river runs free—
(In a land)
Through the green country—
(In a land)
To a shining sea.

And you and me
Are free to be
You and me.

Music by Stephen Lawrence
Lyric by Bruce Hart

For a land
Where the river runs free—
(For a land)
Through the green country—
(For a land)
To a shining sea—
(For a land)
Where the horses run free.

And you and me
Are free to be
You and me.

Every boy in this land
Grows to be his own man.
In this land, every girl
Grows to be her own woman.

Take my hand. Come with me,
Where the children are free.
Come with me. Take my hand,
And we'll run . . .

To a land
Where the river runs free—
(To a land)
Through the green country—
(To a land)
To a shining sea—
(To a land)
Where the horses run free—
(To a land)
Where the children are free.

And you and me
Are free to be
You and me.

And you and me
Are free to be
You and me.

Free To Be . . . a Family

Words by Sarah Durkee, Music by Paul Jacobs
Illustrated by Susan Jeffers

♪ music on page 209

We're all branches of the same big family tree,
but every family's different, don't you know?
Reachin' for the sun comes very naturally.
We've only got to let each other grow!

I've got a home . . .
I've found my place . . .
I live with people who are glad to see my face.

We're free to be . . .
you and me,
and you and me,
we're free to be . . . a family!

We're all workin' in the same big marching band,
but drums and horns have different things to say.
All together we'll ring music through the land
We've only got to let each other play!

I've got a place . . .
I've found my home . . .
I'm only solo when I want to be alone.

We're free to be . . .
you and me,
and you and me,
we're free to be . . . a family!

So many groups in the family soup,
So many combinations,
Might be people who look like you
or they might be no relation!
Birds of a feather, they flock together,
Yes, sometimes they do.
But if a little bird joins an elephant herd,
Hey, that's a family, too!

We're all cookin' up the same big barbeque,
but we like spicy, you like sticky sweet.
Maybe we can trade our recipe with you.
Then how about we help each other eat?!

This is my home . . .
These are my folks . . .
These are our secrets and our habits
    and our jokes.

We're free to be . . .
you and me,
and you and me,
we're free to be . . . a family!

Boy Meets Girl

by Peter Stone and Carl Reiner

DEEP VOICE: Hi!

HIGH VOICE: Hi.

DEEP VOICE: I'm a baby.

HIGH VOICE: What do you think I am, a loaf of bread?

DEEP VOICE: You could be—what do I know? I'm just born. I'm a baby. I don't even know if I'm under a tree or in a hospital or what. I'm just so glad to be here.

HIGH VOICE: Well, I'm a baby, too.

DEEP VOICE: Have it your own way. I don't want to fight about it.

HIGH VOICE: What are you, scared?

DEEP VOICE: Yes, I am. I'm a little scared. I'll tell you why. See, I don't know if I'm a boy or a girl yet.

HIGH VOICE: What's that got to do with it?

DEEP VOICE: Well, if you're a boy and I'm a girl you can beat me up. Do you think I want to lose a tooth my first day alive?

HIGH VOICE: What's a tooth?

DEEP VOICE: Search me. I'm just born. I'm a baby. I don't know nothing yet.

HIGH VOICE: Do you think you're a girl?

DEEP VOICE: I don't know. I might be. I think I am. I've never been anything before. Let me see. Let me take a little look around. Hmm. Cute feet. Small, dainty. Yup, yup, I'm a girl. That's it. Girltime.

HIGH VOICE: What do you think I am?

DEEP VOICE: You? That's easy—you're a boy.

HIGH VOICE: Are you sure?

DEEP VOICE: Of course I'm sure. I'm alive already four, five minutes and I haven't been wrong yet.

HIGH VOICE: Gee, I don't feel like a boy.

DEEP VOICE: That's because you can't see yourself.

HIGH VOICE: Why? What do I look like?

DEEP VOICE: Bald. You're bald fellow. Bald, bald, bald. You're bald as a ping-pong ball. Are you bald!

HIGH VOICE: So?

DEEP VOICE: So, boys are bald and girls have hair.

HIGH VOICE: Are you sure?

DEEP VOICE: Of course, I'm sure. Who's bald, your mother or your father?

HIGH VOICE: My father.

DEEP VOICE: I rest my case.

HIGH VOICE: Hmm. You're bald, too.

DEEP VOICE: You're kidding!

HIGH VOICE: No, I'm not.

DEEP VOICE: Don't look!

HIGH VOICE: Why?

DEEP VOICE: A bald girl—blech!—disgusting!

HIGH VOICE: Maybe you're a boy and I'm a girl.

9

DEEP VOICE: There you go again. I told you—I'm a girl. I know it. I know it. I'm a girl, and you're a boy.

HIGH VOICE: I think you're wrong.

DEEP VOICE: I am never wrong! What about shaving?

HIGH VOICE: What about it?

DEEP VOICE: You just shaved, right?

HIGH VOICE: Wrong.

DEEP VOICE: Exactly! And you know why? Because everyone's born with a clean shave. It's just that girls keep theirs and boys don't.

HIGH VOICE: So, what does that prove?

DEEP VOICE: Tomorrow morning, the one that needs a shave, he's a boy.

HIGH VOICE: I can't wait until tomorrow morning.

DEEP VOICE: See? That proves it. Girls are patient, boys are impatient.

HIGH VOICE: Yeh? What else?

DEEP VOICE: Can you keep a secret?

HIGH VOICE: Absolutely.

DEEP VOICE: There you go— boys keep secrets, girls don't.

HIGH VOICE: Go on.

DEEP VOICE: Are you afraid of mice?

HIGH VOICE: No.

DEEP VOICE: I am. I'm terrified of them. I hate them. Squeak. Squeak. Squeak. What do you want to be when you grow up?

lawyer

HIGH VOICE: A fireman.

DEEP VOICE: What'd I tell you?

HIGH VOICE: How about you?

singer

DEEP VOICE: A cocktail waitress. Does that prove anything to you?

HIGH VOICE: You must be right.

DEEP VOICE: I told you—I'm always right. You're a boy and I'm the girl.

HIGH VOICE: I guess so. Oh, wait—here comes the nurse to change our diapers.

DEEP VOICE: About time, too—I have never been so uncomfortable in my life.

HIGH VOICE: Hey—look at that!

DEEP VOICE: What?

HIGH VOICE: You see that? I *am* a girl—and you're a boy!

DEEP VOICE: Hey—it sure looks like it.

HIGH VOICE: What do you think of that?

DEEP VOICE: I can't understand it.

HIGH VOICE: Well, it sure goes to show you.

DEEP VOICE: What?

HIGH VOICE: You can't judge a book by its cover.

DEEP VOICE: Ha. Ha. Ha. What does that mean?

HIGH VOICE: How should I know? I'm only a baby.

DEEP VOICE: So am I. Goo.

HIGH VOICE: Goo.

Boy Meets Girl Plus One

by Peter Stone
Illustrated by Tom Cooke

The Place: A Park
The Time: One month later

BOY: Hi!

GIRL: Are you speaking to me?

BOY: I certainly am. Hi! Hi! Hi, there!

GIRL: Look, just because we're in the park and it's a beautiful day and I'm only a month old and I'm adorable, that doesn't give you the right to talk to strangers.

BOY: What strangers? Don't you remember me? The Hospital? Four weeks ago? That suave, debonaire baby in the next basket?

GIRL: You mean . . .

BOY: Right! The bed wetter!

GIRL: Oh my goodness, of course! The one who thought he was a girl.

BOY: Well, I was wrong. I'm a boy.

GIRL: Are you sure this time?

BOY: Oh, yeah. I'm a boy.

GIRL: How can you tell?

BOY: I hate girls. Boy, I really hate 'em! They're disgusting! Blechhh! All except Brooke Shields. What a cutie. A real strawberry shortcake. *Crazy* about Brooke Shields! You can have all the rest.

GIRL: *I'm* a girl.

BOY: You're kidding.

GIRL: Do you hate me?

BOY: Wait a minute—no, I don't think so. Hey, you don't suppose it's a new phase I'm going through, do you? I'm going through so many new phases I don't know which end is up. So how's life been treating you?

GIRL: I'm not sure. I'm only a month old.

BOY: Yeah, me, too. The time really drags when you're just lying here, doesn't it? When you think there could be seventy, eighty more years of this, it could get to be a real bummer. What's it like where you live?

GIRL: Things'd be really great if it weren't for two things.

BOY: Yeah? What?

GIRL: My brother and sister.

BOY: What's a brother and sister?

GIRL: You know—people who go around pinching you and sticking their tongues out at you and going *PHUTTT!*
　　(Bronx cheer)

BOY: I never heard of such a thing. Why don't you tell them to stop?

GIRL: Are you crazy? I can't talk yet!

BOY: Right. Right. I forgot.

GIRL: Why do you suppose they keep doing those things? I'm not mad at them.

BOY: If you ask me, they're just jealous.

GIRL: Of what?

BOY: Everything! They've got to walk to the park and you get to ride—they've got all those ugly white things in their mouth and you don't—they've got to get up to go to the bathroom and you can do it right where you are—

GIRL: You know something? I think you're right.

BOY: I'm always right. It's a curse. I've been alive one month and already I've been right five times. A *curse*!

GIRL: You were wrong about being a girl . . .

BOY: That was my first try. You get one practice wrong before it counts. What'd you call those terrible people—brother and what?

GIRL: Sister.

BOY: I never heard of such a thing. Where did they come from?

GIRL: I don't know. They were already there when I got home. I think maybe my mother gave birth to them—like she gave birth to me.

BOY: My mother didn't give birth to *any* children. Not even me.

GIRL: What do you mean?

BOY: I was adopted.

GIRL: What's that?

BOY: Remember when your family came to get you at the hospital?

GIRL: Of course.

BOY: Mine let their fingers do the walking.

GIRL: I don't understand.

BOY: They sent away.

GIRL: That sounds weird.

BOY: Are you kidding? It's great! Think of the adventure. They could've ended up with *any*body—a blond one, a dark one, a fat one, a skinny one, one with a dimple, one with a rosebud for a mouth, one with a cute little tush—but what did they get? All of it—me! Your family *had* to take you, no matter what.

GIRL: They didn't do so bad.

BOY: Believe me, you're not such a hot item.

GIRL: That's an awful thing to say!

BOY: What do you expect? I'm too young to be diplomatic. I call 'em like I see 'em.

GIRL: Look—here comes another baby carriage.

16

NEW GIRL: What you say, momma? What's goin' down, my main man? Gimme five and that's no jive!

BOY: Look at that—a baby basketball player.

NEW GIRL: Look at *that*—a baby baseball manager.

BOY: What makes you think I'm a baseball manager?

NEW GIRL: What makes you think I'm a basketball player?

BOY: I'm sorry. It's just that I saw you dribbling.
    (Explaining)
That's a little joke, you see.

NEW GIRL: Hey, fool, how'd you like me to put one upside your head?

BOY: I don't think I'd like that at all.

GIRL: You're *always* making jokes. I'll bet you want to be a comedian when you grow up.

BOY: No, I want to be the same thing my father is. He's an anchorperson.

GIRL: No kidding! Have I seen him? What's he on?

BOY: The *S.S. Morris Greenblatt.*

NEW GIRL: What channel's that?

BOY: The East River.

NEW GIRL: He's an anchorperson on the *East River*?

BOY: Certainly! When the captain shouts "Anchors aweigh!" he pulls it up and off we go.

NEW GIRL: That's all he does?

BOY: What do you mean? It happens to be a very important job. If he didn't do it, the boat couldn't go anywhere. Of course, it means he has to be away from home a lot. But when I *do* see him, he gives me quality time. That's my favorite thing, quality time—that and holding someone's finger.

NEW GIRL: When *I* grow up, I'm gonna be the same thing my *momma* is.

BOY: What's that?

NEW GIRL: A cocktail waitress.

BOY: A cocktail waitress! You're kidding! That's what *I* wanted to be! Before I decided to be an anchorperson, of course.
    (Confidentially)
I'll tell you the truth—I *still* want to be a cocktail waitress. That cute little tray, those fishnet stockings, all those tips—oo*ee*!
    (Once again talking to NEW GIRL)
        And how 'bout your *dad*? Is he a cocktail waitress, too?

NEW GIRL: No, he's a dentist.

BOY: A *what*?

NEW GIRL: A dentist. You know—a person you go to when you need your teeth fixed.

BOY: What are teeth?

NEW GIRL: I don't know. They show up later. But if you don't brush 'em twice a day, they go away again.

BOY: Okay, so what we've got here so far, job-wise, is a cocktail waitress, an anchorperson and a dentist. Now what about you?

GIRL: Me? You're talking to me?

BOY: You bet your cute booties. So tell me, what do *your* parents do?

GIRL: Well . . . my mother drives a truck.

BOY: You're kidding! Your mother drives a *truck*?

GIRL: You want to make something of it?

BOY: Well, no, I don't think I do.

GIRL: You want me to put something up—uh—next to your head?

NEW GIRL: Upside your head, darlin'—upside.

GIRL: Yeah, upside your head.

BOY: What are you getting so excited about? I think truck drivers are great! If I can't be an anchorperson or a cocktail waitress, I'm going to drive a truck.

NEW GIRL: And what about your father, darlin'? What's he do?

GIRL: *(Hesitates)* What's a father?

NEW GIRL: You know . . .

GIRL: No, I don't.

NEW GIRL: Sure you do. Remember when you were being born and everybody was running around like crazy and people were doing all sorts of weird stuff, remember that?

GIRL: Yeah . . .

NEW GIRL: Well, the one who was getting nauseous is called a father.

GIRL: We don't have one of them. There's just my mother and my brother and my sister and me.

BOY: That's terrible.

GIRL: No it's not! We have a *good* time, my mom and me. She feeds me and she plays with me and she hugs me and kisses me and she protects me and she tells me I'm beautiful. I *am* beautiful, don't you think?

18

NEW GIRL: You certainly are. And you want to know why? It's because somebody loves you. It doesn't matter if it's a mom or a pop or a second cousin once removed—long as one person loves you, you're beautiful. That's what my father, the dentist, says.

BOY: Gosh, that's nice. Your father's a regular *philosopher*-dentist.

NEW GIRL: Yeah? What's that?

BOY: How should I know? I'm only one month old.

GIRL: Hey, you know what let's do? Why don't we meet here in the park every day for the rest of our lives?

BOY: Every day? Let me check—I think my calendar's clear. Monday . . . Tuesday . . . yep, every day's fine. How about you?

NEW GIRL: Why not? I got nothin' better to do till I can walk.

GIRL: Okay, then. It's a date.

BOY: My first date! I'm so excited I could stop wetting my pants.

GIRL: I'll bring the apple juice.

NEW GIRL: I'll bring the strained carrots.

BOY: And I'll bring the ribs.

NEW GIRL: What do you know about ribs, fool?

GIRL: Hey, look out. Here come some grown-ups.

NEW GIRL: Uh oh. We don't want *them* messin' in.

BOY: There's only one thing to do. Ready?

GIRL: Ready.

BOY: Goo!

GIRL: Goo!

NEW GIRL: Goo, baby.

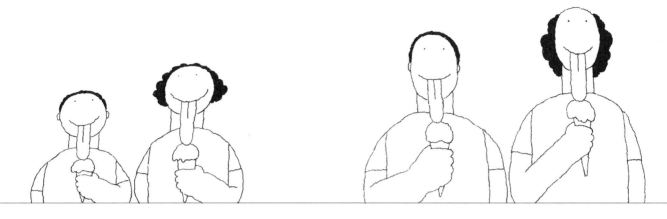

When We Grow Up

Music by Stephen Lawrence, Lyric by Shelley Miller

♪ see page 220 for the music

When we grow up will I be pretty?
Will you be big and strong?
Will I wear dresses that show off my knees?
Will you wear trousers twice as long?

Well, I don't care if I'm pretty at all
And I don't care if you never get tall
I like what I look like and you're nice small
We don't have to change at all.

When we grow up will I be a lady?
Will you be on the moon?
Well, it might be all right to dance by its light
But I'm gonna get up there soon.

Well, I don't care if I'm pretty at all
And I don't care if you never get tall
I like what I look like and you're nice small
We don't have to change at all.

When I grow up I'm going to be happy
And do what I like to do,
Like making noise and making faces
And making friends like you.

And when we grow up do you think we'll see
That I'm still like you
And you're still like me?
I might be pretty
You might grow tall
But we don't have to change at all.

Ladies First

by Shel Silverstein
adapted by Mary Rodgers

Did you hear the one about the little girl who was a "tender sweet young thing?" Well, that's the way she thought of herself. And this tender sweet young thing spent a great deal of time just looking in the mirror, saying,

"I am a *real* little lady.
Anybody could tell that:

When she was at the end of the lunch line at school, all she had to say was,

CAFETERIA

"Ladies first, ladies first!"

and she'd get right up to the front of the line.

Well, her life went on like that
for quite awhile and she wound up
having a pretty good time—you know
—admiring herself in mirrors,
always getting to be first in line,
and stuff like that.

And then one day she went exploring with a whole group of other people through the wilds of a deep and beastly jungle. As she went along through the tangled trails and the prickly vines, she would say things like,

"I have got to be careful of my lovely
dress and my nice white socks
and my shiny, shiny shoes
and my curly, curly locks,
so
would somebody please
clear the way for me?"

And they did.

Or sometimes she'd say,

"What do you *mean* there aren't enough mangoes to go around
and I'll have to share my mango
because I was the last one across that icky river
full of crocodiles and snakes?
No matter how last I am,
it's still
'Ladies first, ladies first.'
so
hand over a whole mango, please."

And they did.

Well, then, guess what happened? Out of nowhere, the exploring party was seized, grabbed up by a bunch of hungry tigers, and these tigers tied all the people up and dragged them back to their tiger lair where they sniffed around, trying to decide what would make the best dinner.

"How about this one?"

said the tiger chief.

"Naah, too bony,"

said the others.

"What about this one? It's got a lotta meat on it."

"Uh-unh, meaty, but muscle-y."

25

"I'm also a little lady.
You should know that by my lovely clothes and my
lovely smell. And if it's all the same to you, Tiger Tweetie,
I wish you'd stop licking me and untie me, this instant.
My dress is getting mussed."

"Yes . . . Well as a matter of fact, we were all just trying to decide who to
untie first."

"*Ladies* first, *ladies* first,"   she said.

And so she was.

B U R P !,!,!

And mighty tasty, too!

Don't Dress Your Cat in an Apron

by Dan Greenburg

Don't dress your cat in an apron
Just 'cause he's learning to bake.
Don't put your horse in a nightgown
Just 'cause he can't stay awake.
Don't dress your snake in a muu-muu
Just 'cause he's off on a cruise.
Don't dress your whale in galoshes
If she really prefers overshoes.

A person should wear what he wants to
And not just what other folks say.
A person should do what she likes to—
A person's a person that way.

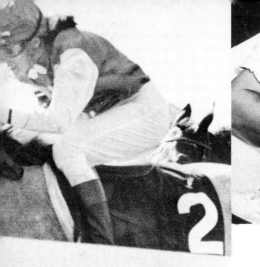

Parents Are People

♪ music on page 216

Mommies are people.
People with children.
When mommies were little
They used to be girls,
Like some of you,
But then they grew.

And now mommies are women,
Women with children,
Busy with children
And things that they do.
There are a lot of things
A lot of mommies can do.

Some mommies are ranchers
Or poetry makers
Or doctors or teachers
Or cleaners or bakers.
Some mommies drive taxis
Or sing on TV.
Yes, mommies can be
Almost anything they want to be.

They can't be grandfathers . . .
Or daddies . . .

Daddies are people.
People with children.
When daddies were little
They used to be boys,
Like some of you,
But then they grew.

And now daddies are men,
Men with children,
Busy with children
And things that they do.
There are a lot of things
A lot of daddies can do.

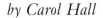

by Carol Hall

Some daddies are writers
Or grocery sellers
Or painters or welders
Or funny joke tellers.
Some daddies play cello
Or sail on the sea.
Yes, daddies can be
Almost anything they want to be.

They can't be grandmas . . .
Or mommies . . .

Parents are people.
People with children.
When parents were little
They used to be kids,
Like all of you.
But then they grew.

And now parents are grown-ups,
Grown-ups with children,
Busy with children
And things that they do.
There are a lot of things
A lot of mommies
And a lot of daddies
And a lot of parents
Can do.

Housework

by Sheldon Harnick

You know, there are times
  when we happen to be
just sitting there quietly
  watching TV,
when the program we're watching

  will stop for awhile
and suddenly someone
  appears with a smile
and starts to show us
  how terribly urgent
it is to buy some brand
  of detergent
    or soap
    or cleanser
    or cleaner
    or powder
    or paste

or wax
or bleach—
to help with the housework.

Now, most of the time
it's a lady we see
who's doing the housework
on TV.
She's cheerfully scouring
a skillet or two,
or she's polishing pots
'til they gleam like new,

or she's scrubbing the tub,
or she's mopping the floors,
or she's wiping the stains
from the walls and the doors,
or she's washing the windows,
the dishes, the clothes,
or waxing the furniture
'til it just glows,
or cleaning the "fridge,"
or the stove or the sink
with a lighthearted smile
and a friendly wink

and she's doing her best
   to make us think
that *her* soap
      or detergent
      or cleanser
      or cleaner
      or powder
      or paste
      or wax
      or bleach
is the best kind of soap
      (or detergent

      or cleanser
      or cleaner
      or powder
      or paste
      or wax
      or bleach)
that there is in the whole wide world!

And maybe it is . . .
and maybe it isn't . . .
and maybe it does what they
   say it will do . . .

but I'll tell you one thing
   I *know* is true:

The lady we see
   when we're watching TV—
The lady who smiles
  as she scours
        or scrubs
        or rubs
        or washes
        or wipes
        or mops

        or dusts
        or cleans—
or whatever she does
on our TV screens—
that lady is smiling
because she's an actress.
And she's earning money
for learning those speeches
that mention those wonderful
        soaps
        and detergents
        and cleansers

and cleaners
and powders
and pastes
and waxes
and bleaches.
So the very next time
you happen to be
just sitting there quietly
watching TV,
and you see some nice lady
who smiles as

she scours
or scrubs
or rubs
or washes
or wipes
or mops
or dusts
or cleans
remember:
Nobody smiles doing housework
but those ladies you see on TV.
Because even if

the soap
      or detergent
      or cleanser
      or cleaner
      or powder
      or paste
      or wax
      or bleach
that you use
      is the very best one—
housework

      is just no fun.

Children,
when you have a house of your own
make sure, when there's housework to do,
that you don't have to do it alone.
Little boys, little girls,
when you're big husbands and wives,
if you want all the days of your lives
to seem sunny as summer weather
make sure, when there's housework to do,
that you do it together.

The Pain and

My brother's a pain.
He won't get out of bed
In the morning.
My mother has to carry him
Into the kitchen.
He opens his eyes
When he smells
His Sugar Pops.

He should get dressed
  himself.
He's six.
He's in first grade.
But he's so pokey
Daddy has to help him
Or he'd never be ready
  in time
And he'd miss the bus.

He cries if I
Leave without him.
Then Mom gets mad
And yells at me.
Which is another
  reason why
My brother's a pain.

He's got to be first
To show Mom
His school work.
She says *ooh* and *aah*
Over all his pictures.
Which aren't great at all
But just ordinary
First grade stuff.

At dinner he picks
At his food.
He's not supposed
To get dessert
If he doesn't
Eat his meat.
But he always
Gets it anyway.

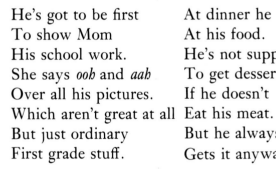

When he takes a bath
My brother the pain
Powders the whole bathroom
And he never gets his face clean.
Daddy says
He's learning to
Take care of himself.
I say,
He's a slob!

Continued on page 40

The Great One

by Judy Blume

My sister thinks she's
  so great
Just because
  she's older.
Which makes Daddy
  and Mom think
She's really smart.
But I know the truth.
My sister's a jerk.

She thinks she's great
Just because she can
Play the piano.
And you can tell
The songs
  are real ones.
But I like
  my songs better.
Even if nobody
Ever heard them before.

My sister thinks she's so great
Just because she can work
The electric can opener.
Which means she gets
To feed the cat.
Which means the cat
Likes her better than me
Just because she feeds her.

My sister thinks she's so great
Just because Aunt Diana lets
Her watch the baby.
And tells her how much
The baby likes *her.*

And all the time
The baby is sleeping
In my dresser drawer.
Which my mother
  has fixed up
Like a bed
For when the baby
Comes to visit.

And I'm not supposed
To touch him
Even if he's
In *my* drawer
And gets changed
On *my* bed.

Continued on page 41

39

The Pain

My brother the pain
Is two years younger than me.
So how come
He gets to stay up
As late as I do?
Which isn't really late enough
For somebody in third grade
Anyway.

I asked Mom and
    Daddy about that.
They said,
"You're right.
You *are* older.
You *should* stay
    up later."

So they tucked the Pain
Into bed.
I couldn't wait
For the fun to begin.
I waited
And waited
And waited.
But Daddy and Mom
Just sat there
Reading books.

Finally I shouted,
"I'm going to bed!"

"We thought you wanted
To stay up later,"
They said.

"I did.
But without the Pain
There's nothing to do!"

"Remember that tomorrow,"
My mother said.
And she smiled.

Continued on page 42

The Great One

My sister thinks she's so great
Just because she can
Remember phone numbers.
And when she dials
She never gets
The wrong person.

And when she has
  friends over
They build whole cities
Out of blocks.
I like to be garbage man.
I zoom my trucks
  all around.
So what if I
  knock down
Some of the buildings?

"It's not fair
That she always gets
To use
  the blocks!"
I told my mother
  and father.

They said,
"You're right.
Today you can
  use the blocks
All by yourself."

"I'm going to build
  a whole city
Without you!"
I told the Great One.

"Go ahead," she said.
"Go build a whole
  state without me.

See if I care!"

So I did.
I built a whole
  country
All by myself.
Only it's not the
  funnest thing
To play blocks alone.
Because when I
  zoomed my trucks
And knocked down
  buildings
Nobody cared but me!

"Remember that tomorrow,"
Mom said, when I told her
I was through playing blocks.

Continued on page 43

The Pain

But the next day
My brother was
    a pain again.
When I got a phone call
He danced all around me
Singing stupid songs
At the top of his lungs.
Why does he have to
    act that way?
And why does he
    always
Want to be
    a garbage man
When I build a city
Out of blocks?
Who needs him
Knocking down
    buildings
With his dumb
    old trucks!

And I would really like to know
Why the cat sleeps on the Pain's bed
Instead of mine.
Especially since I am the one
Who feeds her.
That is the meanest thing of all!

I don't understand
How my mother can say
The Pain is lovable.
She's always kissing him
And hugging him
And doing disgusting things
Like that.
And my father says
The Pain is just what
They always wanted.

YUCK!

I think they love him better than me.

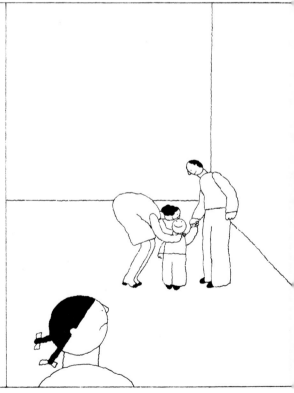

42

But the next day
We went swimming.
I can't stand my sister
When we go swimming.
She thinks she's so great
Just because she can
swim and dive
And isn't afraid
To put her face
In the water.
I'm scared to
put mine in
So she calls me *baby*.

Which is why
I have to
Spit water at her
And pull her hair
And even pinch her
Sometimes.

And I don't think it's fair
For Daddy and Mom to yell at me
Because none of it's my fault.
But they yell anyway.

Then my mother hugs my sister
And messes with her hair
And does other disgusting things
Like that.
And my father says
The Great One is just what
They always wanted.

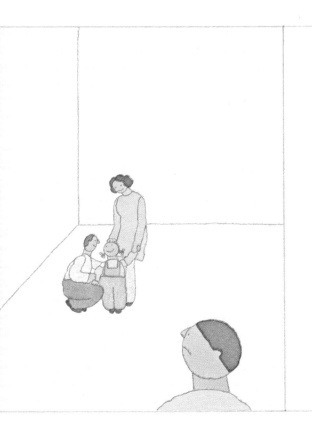

YUCK!

I think they love her better than me.

The Southpaw

by Judith Viorst

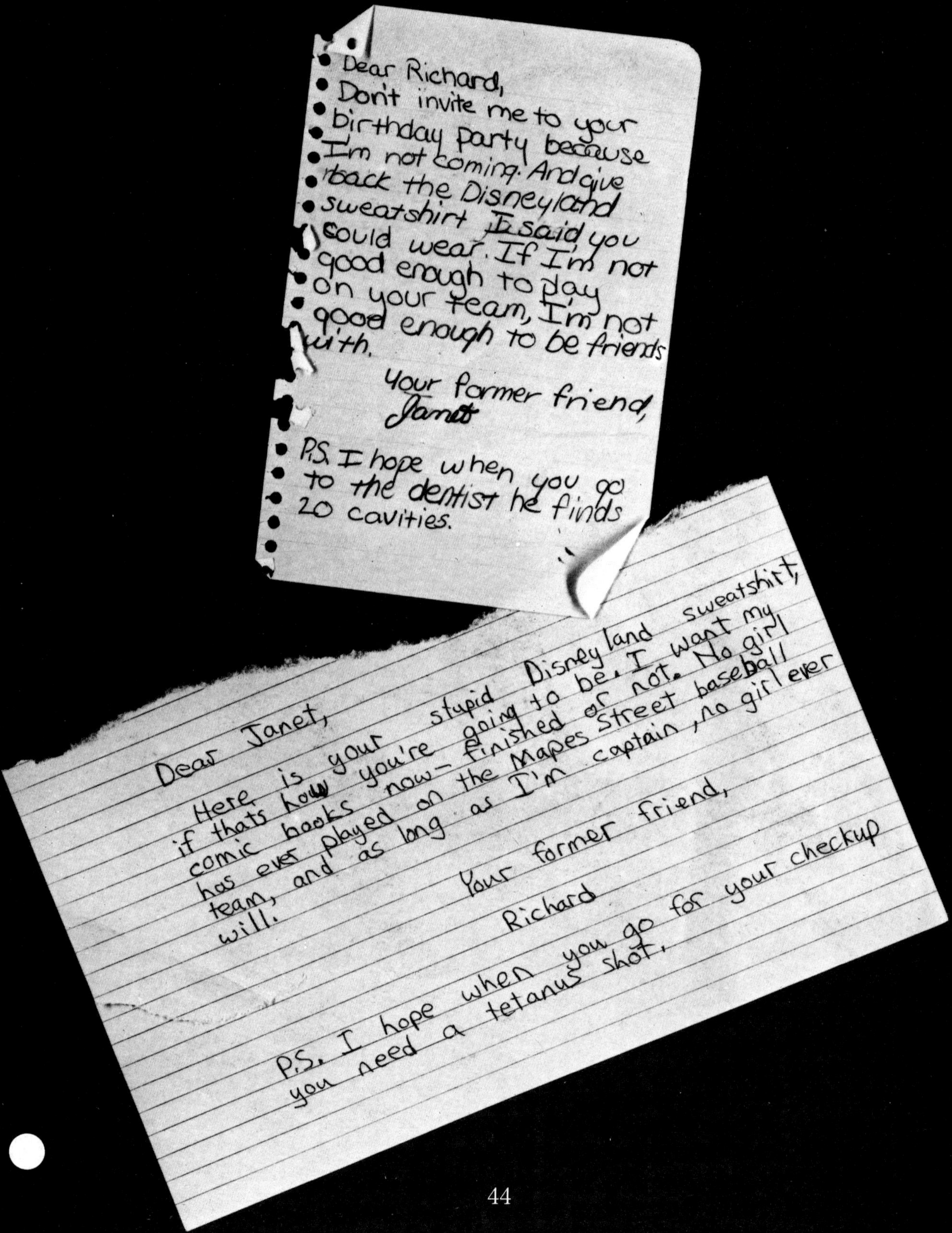

Dear Richard,
Don't invite me to your birthday party because I'm not coming. And give back the Disneyland sweatshirt I said you could wear. If I'm not good enough to play on your team, I'm not good enough to be friends with.

Your former friend,
Janet

P.S. I hope when you go to the dentist he finds 20 cavities.

Dear Janet,
Here is your stupid Disneyland sweatshirt, if thats how you're going to be. I want my comic books now-finished or not. No girl has ever played on the Mapes Street baseball team, and as long as I'm captain, no girl ever will.

Your former friend,
Richard

P.S. I hope when you go for your checkup you need a tetanus shot.

Dear Richard,

I'm changing my goldfish's name from Richard to Stanley. Don't count on my vote for class president next year. Just because I'm a member of the ballet club doesn't mean I'm not a terrific ballplayer.

Your former friend,
Janet

P.S. I see you lost your first game 28-0

Dear Janet,

I'm not saving any more seats for you on the bus. For all I care you can stand the whole way to school. Why don't you just forget about baseball and learn something nice like knitting?

Your former friend,

Richard

P.S. Wait until Wednesday

Dear Richard,

My father said I could call someone to go with us for a ride and hot-fudge sundaes. In case you didn't notice, I didn't call you.

Your former friend,
Janet

P.S. I see you lost your second game, 34-0.

Dear Janet,

Remember when I took the laces out of my blue-and-white sneakers and gave them to you? I want them back.

Your former friend,
Richard

P.S. Wait until Friday.

Dear Richard,
Congratulations on your unbroken record. Eight straight losses, wow! I understand you're the laughingstock of New Jersey.
              Your former friend,
              Janet

P.S. Why don't you and your team forget about baseball and learn something nice like knitting maybe?

Dear Janet,
      Here's the silver horseback riding trophy that you gave me. I don't think I want to keep it anymore.
              Your former friend,
              Richard
P.S. I didn't think you'd be the kind who'd kick a man when he's down.

Dear Richard,
I wasn't kicking exactly. I was kicking back.
      Your former friend,
      Janet

P.S. In case you were wondering, my batting average is .345.

Dear Janet,
      Alfie is having his tonsils out tomorrow. We might be able to let you catch next week.
              Richard

Dear Richard,
I pitch.
Janet

Dear Janet,
Joel is moving to Kansas and Danny sprained his wrist. How about a permanent place in the outfield?
Richard

Dear Richard,
I pitch.
Janet

Dear Janet,
Ronnie caught the chicken pox and Leo broke his toe and Elwood has these stupid violin lessons. I'll give you first base, and that's my final offer.
Richard

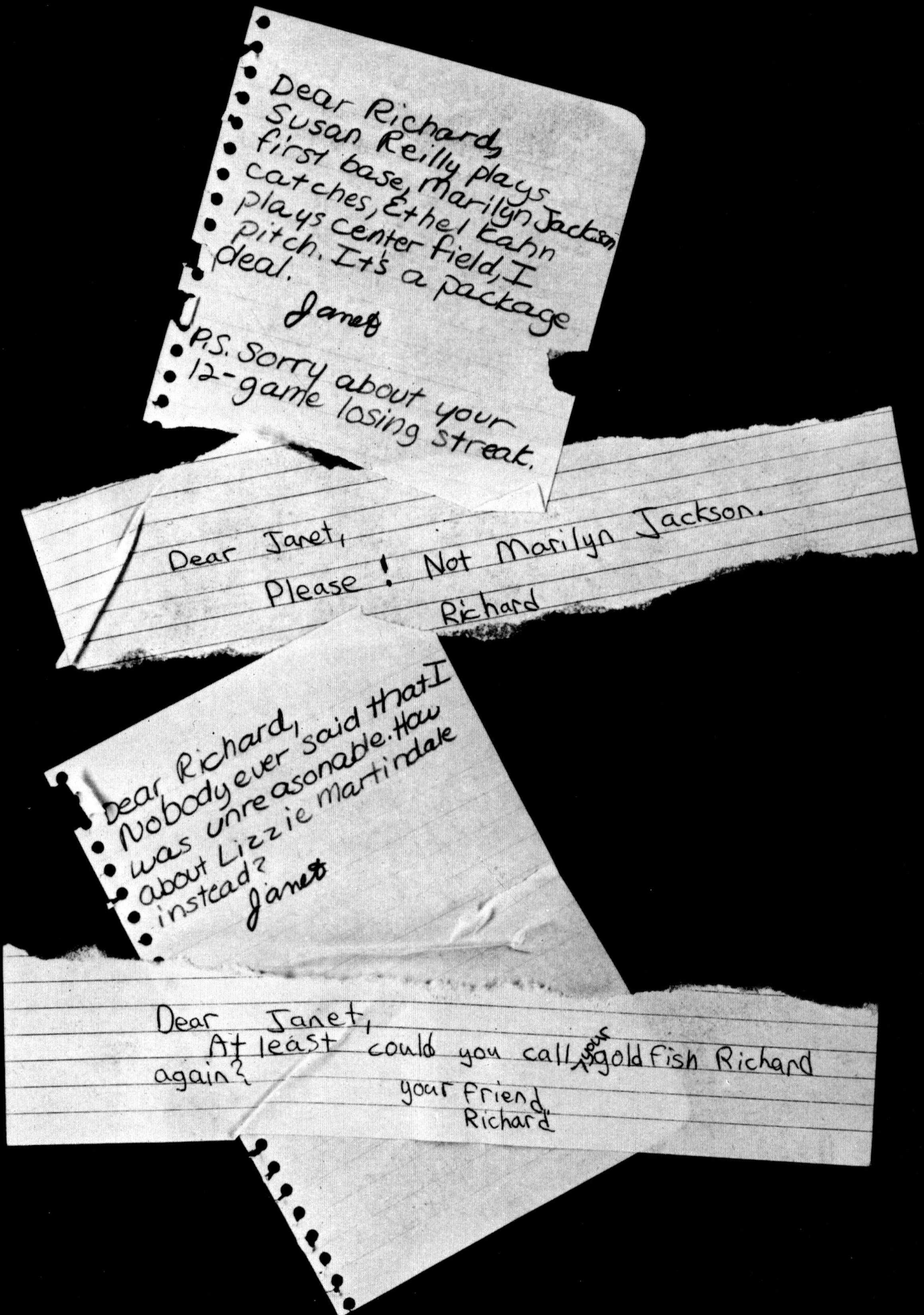

Dear Richard,
Susan Reilly plays first base, Marilyn Jackson catches, Ethel Kahn plays center field, I pitch. It's a package deal.
Janet

P.S. Sorry about your 12-game losing streak.

Dear Janet,
Please! Not Marilyn Jackson.
Richard

Dear Richard,
Nobody ever said that I was unreasonable. How about Lizzie Martindale instead?
Janet

Dear Janet,
At least could you call your goldfish Richard again?
your friend,
Richard

My Dog Is a Plumber

by Dan Greenburg

My dog is a plumber, he must be a boy.
Although I must tell you his favorite toy
Is a little play stove with pans and with pots
Which he really must like, 'cause he plays with it lots.
So perhaps he's a girl, which kind of makes sense,
Since he can't throw a ball and he can't climb a fence.
But neither can Dad, and I know *he's* a man,
And Mom is a woman, and *she* drives a van.
Maybe the problem is in trying to tell
Just what someone is by what he does well.

The Old Woman Who Lived in a Shoe

by Joyce Johnson

There was an old woman
  who lived in a shoe,
And all her grandchildren
  played there too.

She laughed at their jokes
  (when they were funny)
And kept a green jar
  of bubblegum money.
She rode with them
  on the carousel
And played Monopoly
  very well.

She taught them to paint
  and how to bake bread.
She read them riddles
  and tucked them in bed.
She taught them to sing
  and how to climb trees.
She patched their jeans
  and bandaged their knees.

She remembered the way
  she'd felt as a child,
The dreams she'd had
  of lands that were wild,
Of mountains to climb
  of villains to fight,
Of plays and poems
  she'd wanted to write.

She remembered all
  she'd wanted to do
Before she grew up
  and lived in the shoe.

There was an old woman
  who lived in a shoe
And lived in the dreams
  she'd had once too.
She told those she loved,
  "Children be bold.
Then you'll grow up
  But never grow old."

Dudley Pippin and the Principal

by Phil Ressner

One day at school the sand table tipped over. Dudley Pippin's teacher thought Dudley had done it and she made him stay a long time after school. Dudley was very angry. On his way home he met the principal, who had a long nose and fierce eyes.

"Hello, Dudley," the principal said. "People are saying you tipped over the sand table at school today."

Dudley just shook his head, because he couldn't say anything. It wasn't fair.

The principal said, "Didn't you do it?"

Dudley shook his head.

"I *knew* you didn't do it," the principal said. "Your teacher must have made a mistake. It wasn't fair. We'll have to do something about it, first thing tomorrow morning."

Dudley nodded.

"I bet you'd like to cry," the principal said.

"No," Dudley said, and began to cry. "Boo-wah, hoo-wah," he cried. "Boo-hooh, wah-hoo, boo-hoo-wah." He cried a long time.

"That's fine," the principal said when Dudley was through.

"I'm sorry," Dudley said.

"What for?" the principal said. "You did that very well."

"But only sissies cry," Dudley said.

"A sissy," the principal said, "is somebody who *doesn't* cry because he's afraid people will call him a sissy if he *does.*"

"I'm all mixed up." Dudley said.

"Of course," the principal said. "Why should *you* be any different from everybody else? Most people spend their whole lives trying to get unmixed up."

Then he took a little blue flute out of his pocket. "Say," he said. "Just listen to this nice tune I learned yesterday; it's lovely."

And he began to play, and the music was sad and joyous and it filled the quiet street and went out over the darkling trees and the whole world.

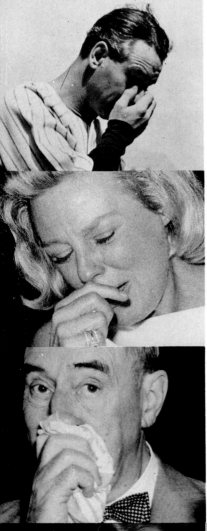

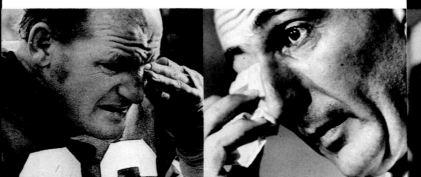

It's All Right to Cry

by Carol Hall

♪ music on page 223

It's all right to cry
Crying gets the sad out of you.
It's all right to cry
It might make you feel better.

Raindrops from your eyes
Washing all the mad out of you.
Raindrops from your eyes
It might make you feel better.

It's all right to feel things
Though the feelings may be strange.
Feelings are such real things
And they change and change
And change . . .
Sad and grumpy,
Down in the dumpy
Snuggly huggly,
Mean and ugly
Sloppy slappy,
Hoppy happy
Change and change and change . . .

It's all right to know
Feelings come and feelings go.
And it's all right to cry
It might make you feel better.

No One Else

by Elaine Laron
drawings by Daniel Pinchbeck, age 7

Now, someone else can tell you how
To multiply by three
And someone else can tell you how
To spell Schenectady
And someone else can tell you how
To ride a two-wheeled bike
But no one else, no, no one else
Can tell you what to like.

An engineer can tell you how
To run a railroad train
A map can tell you where to find
The capital of Spain
A book can tell you all the names
Of every star above
But no one else, no, no one else
Can tell you who to love.

Your aunt Louise can tell you how
To plant a pumpkin seed
Your cousin Frank can tell you how
To catch a centipede
Your Mom and Dad can tell you how
To brush between each meal
But no one else, no, no one else
Can tell you how to feel.

For how you feel is how you feel
And all the whole world through
No one else, no, no one else
Knows *that* as well as YOU!

Three Wishes

by Lucille Clifton

Everybody knows there's such a thing as luck. Like when a good man be the first person to come in your house on the New Year Day you have a good year, but I know somethin better than that! Find a penny on the New Year Day with your birthday on it, and you can make three wishes on it and the wishes will come true! It happened to me.

First wish was when I found the penny. Me and Victorius Richardson was goin for a walk, wearin our new boots we got for Christmas and our new hat and scarf sets when I saw somethin all shiny in the snow.

Victor say, "What is that, Lena?"

"Look like some money," I say, and I picked it up. It was a penny with my birthday on it. 1962.

Victor say, "Look like you in for some luck now, Lena. That's a lucky penny for you. What you gonna wish?"

"Well, one thing I do wish is it wasn't so cold," I say just halfway jokin. And the sun come out. Just then.

Well, that got me thinkin. Me and Victor started back to my house both of us thinkin bout the penny and what if there really is such a thing and what to wish in case. Mama was right in the living room when we got to the house.

"How was the walk, Nobie?"

"Fine thank you, Mama," I say.

"Fine thank you, ma'am," Victor say as we went back to the kitchen.

My name is Zenobia after somebody in the Bible. My name is Zenobia and everybody calls me Nobie. Everybody but Victor. He calls me Lena after Lena Horne and when I get grown I'm goin to Hollywood and sing in the movies and Victorius is gonna go with me 'cause he my best friend. That's his real name.

Back in the kitchen it was nice and warm 'cause the stove was lit and Mama had opened the oven door. Me and Victor sat at the table talkin soft so nobody would hear.

"You get two more wishes, Lena."

"You really think there's somethin to it?"

"What you mean, didn't you see how the sun come ridin out soon as you said about it bein too cold?"

"You really think so?"

60

"Man, don't you believe nothin?"

"I just don't believe everything like you do, that's all!"

"Well, you just simple!"

"Who you callin simple?"

"Simple you, that's who, simple Zenobia!"

I jumped up from the table, "Man, I wish you would get out of here!" and Victor jumped up and ran out of the room and grabbed his coat and ran out of the house. Just then.

Well, I'm tellin you! I just sat back down at the table and shook my head. I had just about wasted another wish! I didn't have but one more left!

Mama came into the kitchen lookin for me. "Zenobia, what was the matter with Victorius?" She call me Zenobia when she kind of mad.

"We was just playin, Mama."

"Well, why did he run out of here like that?"

"I don't know Mama, that's how Victor is."

"Well, I hope you wasn't bein unfriendly to him Zenobia, 'cause I know how you are too."

"Yes, ma'am. Mama, what would you wish for if you could have anything you wanted in the whole wide world?"

Mama sat down at the table and started playin with the salt shaker. "What you mean, Nobie?"

"I mean, if you could have yourself one wish, what would it be for?"

Mama put the salt back on a straight line with the pepper and got the look on her face like when she tellin me the old wise stuff.

"Good friends, Nobie. That's what we need in this world. Good friends." Then she went back to playin with the table.

Well, I didn't think she was gonna say that! Usually when I hear the grown people talkin bout different things they want, they be talkin bout money or a good car or somethin like that. Mama always do come up with a surprise!

I got up and got my coat and went to sit out on the step. I started thinkin bout ole Victor and all the stuff me and him used to do. Goin to the movies and practicin my singin and playin touch ball and stick ball and one time we found a rock with a whole lotta shiny stuff in it look just like a diamond. One time me and him painted a picture of the whole school. He was really a good friend to me. Never told one of my secrets. Hard to find friends like that.

"Wish I still had a good friend," I whispered to myself, holdin the penny real tight and feelin all sorry for myself.

And who do you think come bustin down the street grinnin at me? Just then!

Yeah, there's such a thing as luck. Lot of people think they know different kinds of luck but this thing bout the penny is really real. I know 'cause just like I say, it happened to me.

Glad to Have a Friend Like You

by Carol Hall

♪ music on page 226

Jill told Bill
That it was lots of fun to cook.
Bill told Jill
That she could bait a real fish hook.

    So they made ooey gooey
    Chocolate cake
    Sticky licky
    Sugar top
    And they gobbled it and giggled.
    And they sat by the river
    And they fished in the water
    And they talked
    As the squirmy wormies wiggled,
    Singin'

    Glad to have a friend like you,
    Fair and fun and skippin' free.
    Glad to have a friend like you,
    And glad to just be me.

Pearl told Earl
That they could do a secret code.
Earl told Pearl
There was free ice cream when it snowed.

    So they sent funny letters
    Which contained mystery messages
    And nobody knew just how they made it.

And they raised up the window
And they scooped all the snow together,
Put milk and sugar in and ate it,
Singin'

    Glad to have a friend like you,
    Fair and fun and skippin' free.
    Glad to have a friend like you,
    And glad to just be me.

Peg told Greg
She liked to make things out of chairs.
Greg told Peg
Sometimes he still hugged teddy bears.

    So they sneaked in the living room
    And piled all the pillows up
    And made it a rocket ship
    To fly in.
    And the bears were their girls and boys
    And they were the astronauts
    Who lived on the moon
    With one pet lion,
    Singin'

    Glad to have a friend like you,
    Fair and fun and skippin' free.
    Glad to have a friend like you,
    And glad to just be me.

Zachary's Divorce

by Linda Sitea

On this particular Saturday morning Zachary's toes woke up first. They wiggled and wiggled and wiggled in the warm sunlight streaming through the windows. Zachary could feel them wiggling but he couldn't see them because his eyes were still asleep. Next, his arms and mouth woke up and together gave a gigantic stretch and yawn. The yawn sounded something like this: "Aaarrr." Then his whole body woke up and turned over and over, quickly, and before the last turn was done his eyes opened and Zachary was all awake.

Slowly he climbed out of bed and tiptoed across the rug. He moved carefully, so he wouldn't step on the blue and green flowers, only the purple ones, because purple was his favorite color.

He went straight to Mommy's and Daddy's room. He looked at Mommy sleeping in Mommy's and Daddy's bed. He looked at the wood sculptures he had made in school that were nailed into the wall. He looked at the leafy avocado plant that was almost to the ceiling, just the right size for pretending you were an explorer lost in the jungle. Zachary looked at the bookshelves and the easel and Mommy's paintings. He even looked in the closets and under the bed. Daddy was not there.

Next he went into the bathroom. And while he was there he sang a little song:

La la pee dee
La la pee vee
La la pee gee

Daddy was not in the bathroom.

Zachary slid down the stairs on his stomach, bump bump, bump.

He walked back and forth from the living room to the dining room four times and tried to practice his whistling. But no whistle came out, only a puff of wind.

Zachary looked at the bookshelves and his favorite plant that was all purple.

Daddy wasn't in the living room either.

Next Zachary went into the kitchen and there on the wall was his best invention. He turned the handle and the pulley went around and the rope pulled the refrigerator door open. Daddy had helped him build it but it was all his own idea. Daddy and Mommy had said it was a really great idea because you could open the refrigerator door without walking all the way over to it. Zachary closed the door now. He didn't feel like any orange juice this morning. No Daddy in the kitchen.

Zachary went back into the living room and sat on the big chair. He pulled Mommy's patchwork quilt over him and settled in. It was usually a very happy patchwork quilt with every color you could think of in it. But it didn't seem so happy lately.

The morning is a very sad time if you have a divorce, Zachary thought. Having a divorce meant that you woke up in the morning and your Daddy was not there because now Daddy lived in another house. Then Zachary thought of Amy who was in school with him. And he remembered how Amy's divorce meant that she woke up in the morning and her Daddy was there but not her Mommy. He wondered how grown-ups decided which kind of divorce to give you, the Mommy kind or the Daddy kind. Then he tried to figure out, if he could choose, which he would rather have, the Mommy kind or the Daddy kind. But it gave him a headache just to think about it.

Zachary stared out the window. "The morning is a very sad time when you have a divorce," Zachary said out loud.

"I know how you feel. Sometimes the morning is very sad for me too," said Mommy, standing on the bottom step. Mommy was wearing her blue T-shirt and the dungarees Zachary liked best of all—the ones with the bright purple paint on them.

Mommy came and cuddled into the big chair with Zachary and pulled the patchwork quilt over her too.

Zachary whispered, "Mommy tell me the story again about why I got a divorce."

Mommy hugged Zachary very hard and then said: "It's not your divorce Zachary, it's Daddy's and mine. We decided we would be happier if we lived apart from each other. You mustn't think it's because of anything you did wrong, because it isn't. Daddy and I have always loved you very much and always will. And remember, you see Daddy a lot and sleep over at his house a lot too."

Zachary snuggled closer to Mommy.

"Do you think Daddy is sometimes sad in the morning too?" Zachary asked.

"Yes, I think he is," said Mommy. "It's okay to be sad. This is a very new thing that has happened to us. But really, as time passes, we'll all get used to the divorce and we'll be less and less and less sad."

"Let's go get some orange juice," Zachary shouted, and ran into the kitchen.

As he turned the pulley handle to open the refrigerator, Zachary pretended time was passing with each turn. And with each turn, he told himself that soon he would feel less and less and less sad.

Atalanta

by Betty Miles

Once upon a time, not long ago, there lived a princess named Atalanta, who could run as fast as the wind.

She was so bright, and so clever, and could build things and fix things so wonderfully, that many young men wished to marry her.

"What shall I do?" said Atalanta's father, who was a powerful king. "So many young men want to marry you, and I don't know how to choose."

"You don't have to choose, Father," Atalanta said. "I will choose. And I'm not sure that I will choose to marry anyone at all."

"Of course you will," said the king. "Everybody gets married. It is what people do."

"But," Atalanta told him, with a toss of her head, "I intend to go out and see the world. When I come home, perhaps I will marry and perhaps I will not."

The king did not like this at all. He was a very ordinary king; that is, he was powerful and used to having his own way. So he did not answer Atalanta, but simply told her, "I have decided how to choose the young man you will marry. I will hold a great race, and the winner—the swiftest, fleetest young man of all—will win the right to marry you."

Now Atalanta was a clever girl as well as a swift runner. She saw that she might win both the argument and the race—provided that she herself could run in the race, too. "Very well," she said. "But you must let me race along with the others. If I am

The crowds cheered as the young men and Atalanta began to race across the field. At first they ran as a group, but Atalanta soon pulled ahead, with three of the young men close after her. As they neared the halfway point, one young man put on a great burst of speed and seemed to pull ahead for an instant, but then he gasped and fell back. Atalanta shot on.

Soon another young man, tense with the effort, drew near to Atalanta. He reached out as though to touch her sleeve, stumbled for an instant, and lost speed. Atalanta smiled as she ran on. I have almost won, she thought.

But then another young man came near. This was Young John, running like the wind, as steadily and as swiftly as Atalanta herself. Atalanta felt his closeness, and in a sudden burst she dashed ahead.

Young John might have given up at this, but he never stopped running. Nothing at all, thought he, will keep me from winning the chance to speak with Atalanta. And on he ran, swift as the wind, until he ran as her equal, side by side with her, toward the golden ribbon that marked the race's end. Atalanta raced even faster to pull ahead, but Young John was a strong match for her. Smiling with the pleasure of the race, Atalanta and Young John reached the finish line together, and together they broke through the golden ribbon.

Trumpets blew. The crowd shouted and leaped about. The king rose. "Who is that young man?" he asked.

"It is Young John from the town," the people told him.

"Very well. Young John," said the king, as John and Atalanta stood before him, exhausted and jubilant from their efforts. "You have not won the race, but you have come closer to winning than any man here. And so I give you the prize that was promised—the right to marry my daughter."

Young John smiled at Atalanta, and she smiled back. "Thank you, sir," said John to the king, "but I could not possibly marry your daughter unless she wished to marry me. I have run this race for the chance to talk with Atalanta, and, if she is willing, I am ready to claim my prize."

Atalanta laughed with pleasure. "And I," she said to John, "could not possibly marry before I have seen the world. But I would like nothing better than to spend the afternoon with you."

Then the two of them sat and talked on the grassy field, as the crowds went away. They ate bread and cheese and purple plums. Atalanta told John about her telescopes and her pigeons, and John told Atalanta about his globes and his studies of geography. At the end of the day, they were friends.

On the next day, John sailed off to discover new lands. And Atalanta set off to visit the great cities.

By this time, each of them has had wonderful adventures, and seen marvelous sights. Perhaps some day they will be married, and perhaps they will not. In any case, they are friends. And it is certain that they are both living happily ever after.

A Tale of Three Ralphs

by Miriam Minkowitz
Illustrated by Debra Solomon

Once upon a time there lived a husband and wife who decided that if they ever had children, they would do everything in their power to be the fairest parents in the entire world. "To make sure that we bring up all our children equally fairly," they vowed, "let's make one Golden Rule: EACH CHILD WILL BE TREATED *EXACTLY ALIKE*—WITH ABSOLUTELY *NO EXCEPTIONS*."

Soon the husband and wife had a little baby son. They named him Ralph, and they loved and cherished him very deeply. He grew and grew, and the little family was incredibly happy.

When Ralph was three years old, his parents had a second child. This time it was a baby girl. Remembering their rule to treat each of their children *exactly alike*—with absolutely *no exceptions*—they named her Ralph also. For a moment, they thought about calling her Ralph the Second.

"But that's not *exactly* what we called our first child," protested the husband.

"You're right," agreed the wife. "It wouldn't be fair." So they decided to call the new baby just plain Ralph.

As time went on, no matter what happened, the parents kept their promise to treat each of their children exactly alike. And so, when their first Ralph developed a runny nose, they gave *both* children nose drops. And when their second Ralph fell down while roller-skating, both children went around with bandaged knees until the second Ralph's cut was completely healed.

Finally, when the first Ralph was ten, and the second Ralph was seven, the proud parents had a third child—a beautiful baby daughter. Naturally enough, they named her Ralph, and soon afterward, they brought her home from the hospital. It was then that the husband and wife first began to notice that their decision to treat each of their children *exactly alike*—with absolutely *no exceptions*—was causing a few problems.

For one thing, since they wanted to keep newborn Ralph in diapers, they had to make the other Ralphs wear diapers as well. And, since newborn Ralph couldn't walk,

76

the parents were forced to make the other Ralphs lie around in cribs all day, just like their baby sister did. Well, the older Ralphs were not altogether pleased with this state of affairs, and they objected quite strenuously. "It's not fair," they yelled from their cribs. "It's just not fair."

The parents thought long and hard about their children's complaints. "How could it not be fair?" they wondered. "After all, we've brought up each of our children exactly alike—with absolutely no exceptions." Finally, the wife came up with a plan. "Maybe it would be better," she suggested, "if, instead of treating the older Ralphs the same as newborn Ralph, we did just the opposite."

"That's absolutely *brilliant,* sweetheart!" enthused the husband. "Let's start right away." And they did.

Over the next few weeks, despite both parents' very best efforts to make the new plan a success, matters really didn't improve much. For example, when they demanded that newborn Ralph set the table and clean up her room, she just burst into tears and did nothing. When the mother requested, "Ralph, please let the cat out," the infant just stuck her thumb in her mouth and dribbled. And when the father grasped the baby gently by her shoulder and said, "Ralph, it's time for school!" she just wrapped her tiny hand around one of his fingers and answered, "Goooooo?"

"What shall we do?" sobbed the poor father in despair.

"I don't know!" wailed the poor mother. "We have a Golden Rule that all our children are to be treated *exactly* alike. And we absolutely *insist* on being fair. I'm afraid there's just no solution."

Finally the oldest Ralph said, "Maybe we can help." His parents looked at him blankly.

"Maybe, just maybe, all us children could be treated exactly alike—*except for certain things.*"

"Except for certain things?" mused their father. "What a curious idea!"

"It *does* sound interesting," added their mother. "But how would it work?"

"Well, suppose that you and Dad treated us exactly alike—*except* when it seemed silly to do so," answered their son.

"Sure," his sister chimed in. "Like when Mom and Dad made us both get braces because *your* front teeth were crooked, that was silly. But when they bought each of us identical Venus flytrap plants—and identical little bags of bugs and ants to feed them—well, *that* was fair."

Their mother looked at her husband and nodded. "I see what they mean," she said.

"And while we're at it," the second Ralph said, "it's silly for all of us to be called 'Ralph.' And confusing, too."

"But what can we possibly do about it *now*?" their father wanted to know.

"Well, you could *start* by giving us new names," the first Ralph suggested.

"Fair enough," said their father.

"Well, why *not*?" said their mother. She turned to the first Ralph. "Ralph, what would you like *your* name to be?"

"Well, I've always been rather partial to the name 'Ralph,' " he said.

"Okay . . ." said the mother uncertainly. " 'Ralph' it is." She looked at the second Ralph. "And how about you?" she said. "If you could have any name in the world, what would you pick?"

"No doubt about it," her daughter replied without hesitation. "I'd like to be called 'Ralph.' "

"Uh-huh," said the father. He looked in the crib where his infant daughter lay chewing on the schoolbooks her parents had left there in the vain hope she would finally begin to catch up on her homework. "And I suppose you'd like us to keep calling *you* Ralph, too?"

The baby was too young to answer, of course, but the parents could tell from the glint in her eye that the name "Ralph" suited her just fine.

And so, from that time on, Ralph, Ralph, and their little sister Ralph faced a fair, but somewhat confusing, future in a family with a *new* Golden Rule for bringing up children equally fairly:

"SINCE NO RALPHS ARE
JUST LIKE THEIR SISTERS
AND BROTHERS,
WHAT'S GOOD FOR ONE RALPH
MIGHT BE BAD FOR
THE OTHERS."

Or, in other words,
"TO EACH RALPH BE TRUE."

Friendly Neighborhood

Words by Lynn Ahrens,
Music by Stephen Flaherty
Illustrated by Lonni Sue Johnson

♪ music on page 230

My family began
with Mom and Dad and Sam and me.
Then Mom and Dad divorced,
and, boy, I cried!
'Cause suddenly, instead of four,
my family felt like three,
and it took a little while
'til Sam and me could see
that what we'd really done was multiplied.

Mom got married to a fella
and I got to catch the flowers at the wedding.
Well, we like him,
and we call him Ted the Bear.
Ted has three kids
from when he used to be the husband of Alicia,
and they visit us on weekends,
and he takes us everywhere.
And let me tell you,
We really have to squish into that car.
It's a tight squeeze.

And Dad met Marsha. She's a lawyer.
And I think they're getting married.
Her two kids are both adopted,
and they come from Vietnam.

So that makes Mom and Ted the Bear,
and Dad and Marsha and Alicia,
three new brothers, two new sisters,
and my creepy brother Sam.
I think Sam is still a little shy around girls.
Well, he's just little.
I'm older!

And there's Gram,
good old Gram,
and there's Grandpa Henry,
also Grandma Annie,
plus an extra granny,
'cause now there's Grandma Pam.

And I'm not even counting cousins,
'cause by now there must be dozens.
Some are younger, some are older,
I mean, cousins by the ton!
And as for having aunts and uncles,
well, the list would take me hours,
but at holidays and birthdays,
gee, the crowd is really fun!
Except, of course, you
have to get kissed and hugged
a whole lot more. Ugh!

Mom and Dad are doing fine,
And Sam and me are doing fine,
and, hey, we feel a whole lot better
than I ever thought we would!
I mean, okay, my family split,
but now, the pieces kinda fit . . .
and it's like living in the middle of
a friendly neighborhood!
And you know what?
Best thing of all?
They all like me!

Another Cinderella

by Norman Stiles
Illustrated by Ralph Reese

Once upon a time there lived a girl named Cinderella. Not *that* Cinderella. Another Cinderella.

This Cinderella lived with her really nice stepmother, really nice stepsister, and really nice stepbrother. She was the light of their lives. All they wanted was that Cinderella be as happy as a young girl could be.

From the day Cinderella became part of their family, they bent over backward to "give her space" and to "let her do her own thing." They freely and gladly worked their fingers to the bone to give her anything and everything she needed or wanted, and they never, ever made her do *any* chores.

That's right. No chores! Ever! Never!

Not only didn't she have to lift a finger, they would lift it for her.

She didn't have to clean up her room or put her stuff away or even put the cap back on the toothpaste if she didn't feel like it.

She didn't have to help wash the dishes or dry the dishes or bring her dish to the sink or even *use* a dish if she didn't feel like it.

She could do whatever she wanted to do whenever she wanted to do it and they never butted in.

If she didn't feel like it, she didn't have to go to school.

They did her homework for her.

She could eat whenever she was hungry and they would cook it for her no matter what time of day.

She could go to sleep whenever she wanted to go to sleep and get up whenever she wanted to get up.

She could eat in bed . . . even something with gravy!

Of course, she never, ever had to help clean the cinders out of the fireplace. She liked to watch *them* do that. (That's why they called her Cinderella.)

She had it made. What a life!

So how come she cried all the time?

"Who knows? Maybe it's a phase," her stepmother said. "She'll grow out of it . . . I hope."

Of course they tried to talk to her. "Why are you crying?" they would ask.

"I don't know," Cinderella would sob. "I don't know." And she didn't know why she cried. She just couldn't explain it.

"Hey, come on, stop crying," her stepmother would say. "Go out and have some fun! Here's some money. Buy yourself something."

"Eat something."

"Go see a funny play."

"Have your hair done."

"Have your nails done."

"Have a nice cup of tea."

"Have a nice day."

"Whatever it is, try not to think about it."

"Hold your breath and count to twenty. It works with hiccups, maybe it will work with crying."

"Take a trip."

"Take a ride."

"Take an aspirin."

"Take a hot bath."

"Take off a couple of pounds."

Some of these things worked for a little while, but soon, out of nowhere and for no apparent reason, Cinderella would burst into tears again.

Then, one Friday, Cinderella came home from school and said, "I have a book report to write. It's due on Monday."

"A book report? Over the weekend? Oh! You poor dear!" her stepmother said as she arrived home from work.

"Let me do it for you, Cinderella!" the stepbrother cried.

"No, let me!" the stepsister jumped in.

"No. Me!"

"No! Me!"

They argued back and forth.

"Now, now. No fighting, kids. You *both* can do it for her," said Cinderella's stepmother.

"Yay," they yelled as they jumped around happily.

Cinderella burst into tears.

But this time her stepmother offered something very, very special to soothe her. She showed Cinderella a beautiful designer gown that she had bought for her along with the most beautiful and perfect accessories, including an imported pair of hand-blown glass slippers.

Cinderella stopped crying when her stepmother took her outside to see a golden carriage pulled by two gorgeous horses and attended by two very impressive coachpersons.

"You bought all this for me?" Cinderella asked, blowing her nose.

"Well, I bought the gown and the accessories and the shoes. The coach and the horses and the coachpersons are a rental," her stepmother said proudly. "I did all this for you so you can go to the Prince's Ball at the palace on Sunday night. Maybe the Prince will fall in love with you and marry you and make you happy for ever and ever and then you won't cry all the time."

Cinderella burst into tears. At first everybody thought these were tears of joy. But tears of joy don't usually last from just before supper Friday night until breakfast Sunday morning, with no sign of letting up.

While they worried that Cinderella might cry all day and not be able to go to the ball that night, a great wind began to blow outside their cottage. It

blew louder and louder and stronger, shaking the cottage until finally it blew open the front door and then stopped blowing, all at once.

It was strangely calm and quiet, and they all stared at the open door, not knowing what to expect.

Then, from behind them, they heard, "Made you look! Made you look!"

It was Cinderella's Fairy Godmother. "Came in through the window! I love the unexpected," she said with a twinkle in her eye. "Hi! I'm your Fairy Godmother, and I'm here to help with this crying business."

Everyone was thrilled, including Cinderella. *Especially* Cinderella! It wasn't a lot of fun going through life crying all the time. "How are you going to do it? Wave your magic wand and my crying will stop?" Cinderella wondered.

"No, sweetheart," replied the Fairy Godmother patiently. "I'm good, but I'm not *that* good. And even if I could do that, I'm not sure it would be such a good idea."

"I know. You'll wave your magic wand and bring her a Prince who will make her happy and her crying will stop," offered the stepbrother.

"No. I could conjure up a Prince or two, but it wouldn't work anyway."

"Then you'll wave your wand and bring Cinderella riches beyond her dreams and that will make her crying stop," the stepsister said.

"No. That wouldn't work either."

"Then what *will* you do?" the stepmother demanded impatiently.

"Look," said the Fairy Godmother, "I think that what Cinderella needs is a sense of achievement, a feeling of accomplishment, and the satisfaction that comes from meeting a challenge."

"Oh, I see. You're going to wave your magic wand and give her all that," said the stepmother. "Please hurry. We want the red in her eyes to clear up in time for the ball."

"No. She's going to get all that on her own . . . once she is given some reasonable guidelines and compassionate guidance," the Fairy Godmother said.

"Ah, ha! That must be where the wand comes in," said the stepmother.

"No. That's where *you* come in."

Everyone was very confused. Was she going to use that wand or wasn't she?

She was. And she did. First she waved it and turned the gown into overalls, the glass slippers into work boots, the coach into a pumpkin, and the coachpersons into mice. She left the horses as they were to graze peacefully in the yard.

Everyone except the horses was very upset. A Fairy Godmother wasn't supposed to take things away. What kind of Fairy Godmother was she anyway?

"Relax!" she said. "I'm not finished." And she waved her wand and out of thin air produced a piece of paper and a pencil. It was a very nice piece of paper and a good pencil with a sharp point, but what did a pencil and paper have to do with anything?

The Fairy Godmother explained that she would help Cinderella's stepmother make a list of things Cinderella would have to accomplish before the gown and the other stuff would be restored. If she finished doing everything on the list before it was time to go to the ball, so be it. If not, no ball.

They didn't like it. It didn't sound fair or nice or kind or loving. The Fairy Godmother assured them that it was all of the above. She turned to Cinderella and said, "Just do your best, dear. It will work out. Trust me."

"Okay," Cinderella said in a surprisingly strong voice. "I'll try."

So her stepmother, with the help of the Fairy Godmother, made up the list. It was a pretty long list, too, with things like helping with the breakfast dishes, including bringing her dish to the sink; cleaning up her room by herself; helping with the laundry; etc. She even had to do her book report all by herself.

One by one Cinderella did the things on the list, and as she did, she began to feel and look happier and happier. As the day went by, she didn't cry once. It looked like her Fairy Godmother was right. But Cinderella still hadn't written the book report.

"Let us help her," the stepsister begged.

"No," said the stepmother firmly. "I think we should let her do it by herself."

Cinderella's Fairy Godmother smiled because she knew that Cinderella's stepmother was finally getting the picture.

Cinderella smiled, too, and then she wrote and wrote and paced and paced and wrote and erased and wrote some more and finally, with just one hour left before the ball, she finished the book report. She couldn't believe how good she felt. She had never felt that good in her entire life!

Everyone cheered as her Fairy Godmother waved her wand and restored the gown and the glass slippers and the accessories and the coach and the coachpersons.

Cinderella started to cry.

But this time she knew why. She didn't want to go to the ball if it meant she had to marry the Prince. She didn't feel she was ready to get married. She had a lot of things she wanted to do first, like go to school, learn things, grow, become a person, stuff like that.

Her stepmother agreed with her and promised that one thing she didn't have to do if she didn't feel like doing it was marry someone she didn't feel like marrying. The only things she would be expected to do from now on were things like homework and chores and stuff like *that*.

"This calls for a celebration!" the Fairy Godmother said. "And what better place to celebrate than at a ball! Off you go!"

And off they went.

And they had a great time. Cinderella danced with the Prince and thought he was sort of cute and nice. She wanted to stay late, but she left early because she had school the next day and because her stepmother told her it was time to go home.

She did leave her glass slipper behind with the Prince because it had her name and address inside and she wanted to see him again. Besides, she knew where *he* lived so it was only fair.

Over the years Cinderella grew into a fine young woman who wrote book reports for a living. She and the Prince became very good friends, fell in love, got married, and they had a very nice life together.

Cinderella still cried once in a while but, then, so does everybody.

Little Abigail and the Beautiful Pony

Written and Illustrated by Shel Silverstein

There was a girl named Abigail
Who was taking a drive
Through the country
With her parents
When she spied a beautiful sad-eyed
Grey and white pony.
And next to it was a sign
That said,
FOR SALE—CHEAP.
"Oh," said Abigail,
"May I have that pony?
May I please?"
And her parents said,
"No you may not."
And Abigail said,
"But I MUST have that pony."
And her parents said,
"Well, you can't have that pony,
But you can have a nice butter pecan
Ice cream cone when we get home."
And Abigail said,
"I don't want a butter pecan
Ice cream cone,
I WANT THAT PONY—
I MUST HAVE THAT PONY."
And her parents said,
"Be quiet and stop nagging—
You're *not* getting that pony."
And Abigail began to cry and said,
"If I don't get that pony I'll die."
And her parents said, "You won't die.
No child ever died yet from not getting a pony."
And Abigail felt so bad
That when they got home she went to bed,
And she couldn't eat,
And she couldn't sleep,
And her heart was broken,
And she DID die—
All because of a pony
That her parents wouldn't buy.

(This is a good story
To read to your folks
When they won't buy
You something you want.)

THE PONY
THAT THEY
WOULDN'T
BUY ME.
. TOO LATE!

OH, IF SHE WERE ONLY ALIVE
I WOULD BUY HER A HUNDRED
A HUNDRED PONIES!

OH...
WHAT
FOOLS
WE WERE.

I had to take him out to play with me and my friends.

"Is that your brother, Bobby?" they'd ask me.

"No."

"Is that your cousin?"

"No! He's just my friend and he's stayin' at my house and my mother made me bring him."

"Ha, ha. You gotta baby-sit! Bobby the baby-sitter!"

"Aw, be quiet. Come on, Steve. See! Why you gotta make all my friends laugh for?"

"Ha, ha. Bobby the baby-sitter," my friends said.

"Hey, come on, y'all, let's go play in the park. You comin', Bobby?" one of my friends said.

"Naw, my momma said he can't go in the park cause the last time he went he fell and hurt his knee, with his old stupid self."

And then they left.

"You see? You see! I can't even play with my friends. Man! Come on."

"I'm sorry, Robert. You don't like me, Robert? I'm sorry," Stevie said.

"Aw, be quiet. That's okay," I told him.

One time when my daddy was havin' company I was just sittin' behind the couch just listenin' to them talk and make jokes and drink beer. And I wasn't makin' no noise. They didn't even know I was there!

Then here comes Stevie with his old loud self. Then when my father heard him, he yelled at *me* and told me to go upstairs.

Just cause of Stevie.

Sometimes people get on your nerves and they don't mean it or nothin' but they just bother you. Why I gotta put up with him? My momma only had one kid. I used to have a lot of fun before old stupid came to live with us.

One Saturday Steve's mother and father came to my house to pick him up like always. But they said that they were gonna move away and that Stevie wasn't gonna come back anymore.

So then he left. The next mornin' I got up to watch cartoons and I fixed two bowls of corn flakes. Then I just remembered that Stevie wasn't here.

Sometimes we had a lot of fun runnin' in and out of the house. Well, I guess my bed will stay clean from now on. But that wasn't so bad. He couldn't help it cause he was stupid.

I remember the time I ate the last piece of cake in the breadbox and blamed it on him.

We used to play Cowboys and Indians on the stoop.

I remember when I was doin' my homework I used to try to teach him what I had learned. He could write his name pretty good for his age.

I remember the time we played boogie man and we hid under the covers with Daddy's flashlight.

And that time we was playin' in the park under the bushes and we found these two dead rats and one was brown and one was black.

And him and me and my friends used to cook mickies or marshmallows in the park.

We used to have some good times together.

I think he liked my momma better than his own, cause he used to call his mother "Mother" and he called my momma "Mommy."

Aw, no! I let my corn flakes get soggy thinkin' about him.

He was a nice little guy.

He was kinda like a little brother.

Little Stevie.

I'll Fix Anthony

by Judith Viorst
Illustrated by Arnold Lobel

My brother Anthony
can read books now,

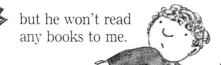

but he won't read
any books to me.

He plays checkers
with Bruce
from his school.
But when
I want to play
he says Go away or I'll clobber you.

I let him wear
my Snoopy sweat shirt,
but he never lets me
borrow his sword.

Mother says deep down
in his heart Anthony loves me.

Anthony says deep down
in his heart he thinks I stink.

Mother says deep deep down
in his heart,
where he doesn't even know it,
Anthony loves me.

Anthony says
deep deep down
in his heart he still thinks I stink.

When I'm six
I'll fix Anthony.

When I'm six a dog
will follow me home,

and she'll beg for me and roll over
and lick my face.

If Anthony tries to pet her,
she'll give him a bite.

When I'm six Anthony will have
the German measles,

and my father will take me
to a baseball game.

Then Anthony will have
the mumps,

and my mother will take me
to the flower show.

Then Anthony will have a virus,
and my grandfather
will take me to the movies.

I won't have to save popcorn
for Anthony unless I want to.

When I'm six we'll have
a skipping contest,
and I'll skip faster.

94

Then we'll have
a jumping contest,
and I'll jump higher.

Then we'll do
Eeny-Meeny-Miney-Mo,
and Anthony will be O-U-T.
He'll be very M-A-D.

When I'm six I'll read

Anthony will still
be reading

Who are you voting for, Anthony?
I'll ask him.

When I'm six I'll stand
on my head,
and my legs won't wobble.

Anthony's legs
will wobble a lot.

If someone tickles me,
I'll keep standing
on my head.

If someone pinches me,
I'll keep standing
on my head.

If someone says
Give up or I'll clobber you,
I'll keep standing on my head.
Anthony will give up at tickles.
When I'm six I'll know
how to sharpen pencils.

Here's how you do it,
Anthony, I'll say.

When I'm six I'll float,
but Anthony will sink
to the bottom.
I'll dive off the board,
but Anthony will change his mind.

I'll breathe in and out when I should,
but Anthony will only go

When I'm six I'll be tall, and Anthony
will be short because I'll eat things
like carrots and potatoes,
and he'll eat things like
jelly beans and root beer.

I'll put his red sneakers
on the top shelf, and if
he stands on a chair,
he still won't be able
to reach them.

He'll tell me
Get down
my sneakers,
and I'll tell him
Say please,

and if he doesn't say
please, he can't have
his sneakers
for a hundred
years.

When I'm six I'll add
    7 and 4 and 10 and 3
    inside my mind.

Anthony will just add 1 and 1 and 2,
and he'll have to use
his fingers.

When I'm six we'll have a race,
and I'll be at the corner when Anthony
hasn't even passed the fireplug.

The next time I'll give him
a head start, but it won't help.

When I'm six friends will call me
on the telephone.

No one will call Anthony.
I'll sleep at Charlie's
house and Eddie's and Diana's, but
Anthony will always sleep at home.

See you later, Anthony, I'll tell him.

When I'm six
I'll help people
carry their groceries
from the supermarket,

and they'll say
My, you're strong.

I don't think Anthony
will be strong enough.

When I'm six
I'll be able to tell
left and right,
but Anthony
will be all mixed up.

I'll be able
to tell time,
but Anthony
will be all mixed up.

I'll be able to tell my street and
my city and sometimes my zip code,
but Anthony will be all mixed up.

If he ever gets lost,
I guess I'll have to go find him.

When I'm six Anthony will still be falling
off his bike.

I'll ride by with no hands.

Still falling off that bike?
I'll ask Anthony.

When I'm six I'll let Dr. Ross
look down my throat
with a stick.

If he has to give me
a shot, I won't
even holler.

Try to be brave like your brother,
Dr. Ross will tell Anthony.

But Anthony won't.

When I'm six my teeth
will fall out,
and I'll put them under the bed,
and the tooth fairy will take
them away and leave dimes.

Anthony's teeth
won't fall out.

He'll wiggle and wiggle them,
but they won't
fall out.

I might sell him one of my teeth,
but I might not.

I'll win all the tic-tac-toes if I'm X,
and I'll win them all if I'm O.
Too bad, Anthony, I'll say.

Anthony is chasing me out
of the playroom.

He says I stink.
He says he is going to clobber me.
I have to run now, but I won't
have to run when I'm six.

When I'm six I'll go BINGO all the time.
Anthony won't even go BINGO once.

When I'm six
I'll fix Anthony.

97

It's Not My Fault

Words and Music by
Sarah Durkee and Christopher Cerf
Illustrated by Gary Zamchick

♪ music on page 225

Mom and Dad are mad tonight,
The dinner table's silent,
My sister's gettin' crabby and
My brother's gettin' violent!
Things are lookin' bad tonight,
It's really plain to see,
And I don't know just who's to blame,
But don't go blamin' *me*!

'Cause it's not my fault!
No, it's not my fault!
My family bit my head off,
And all I said was "Pass the salt!"
Hey, it's not my fault!
No, it's not my fault!
When no one else is talkin',
I just tell myself it's not my fault!

Maybe I should tell a joke,
Make everybody laugh,
But every time I tell one
I forget the second half!
Maybe they're all sick of me
For bein' such a jerk,
Or maybe Dad's just tired,
Maybe Mom's just overworked?

Well, it's not my fault!
No, it's not my fault
That no one's sayin' nothin'
'Cause they don't have nothin' nice to say!
Hey, it's not my fault!
No, it's not my fault!
When no one else is talkin',
I just tell myself that I'm okay!

You might be being perfect,
Might be actin' good as gold,
But sometimes people fight no matter *what* you try to do!
We catch each other's anger
Like we catch each other's cold.
That's when you got to tell yourself it's not because of you!

It's not my fault!
No, it's not my fault!
I know I'm not the one
Who put my family in a rotten mood!
Yeah, it's not my fault!
No, it's not my fault!
And just because we're fighting
Doesn't mean we're gonna come unglued!

Well, it's not my fault!
No, it's not my fault!

Crowded Tub

Written and Illustrated by Shel Silverstein

There's too many kids in this tub.
There's too many elbows to scrub.
I just washed a behind
That I'm sure wasn't mine,
There's too many kids in this tub.

The Entertainer

by Jeff Moss
Illustrated by Chris Demarest

When Elizabeth was not quite three
She learned to say her A–B–C
Both frontward and backward, either way
From A to Z and Z to A.
Well, Lizzie's mom and her father, too,
Were very proud of what Liz could do,
So they gave a small party in their house in the lane
And invited some friends to watch Liz entertain.
"You'll see," said her father, while cutting the cake,
"She'll go forward and backward without a mistake!"
"We're so proud," said her mom, "of our smart little kid.
Say the alphabet, Lizzie!" And Elizabeth did.
She messed up on L and reversed J and K,
And her parents' friends giggled from Z back to A.
And though everyone clapped when young Lizzie was done,
For Liz, the experience wasn't much fun.
"It's strange," Lizzie thought. "They just tell me, 'Go to it!'
But nobody asks me if I *want* to do it."

Well, Elizabeth got to be five or six,
And she learned to do several other tricks.
Her folks gave a party and Lizzie's mom said,
"Guess what, gang! Our Lizzie can stand on her head!
Now everyone watch our remarkable kid.
Okay, stand on your head, Liz!" And Elizabeth did.
She teetered and tottered and didn't quite fall,
And she wished she could just crawl away from it all.
"It's strange," Lizzie thought. "They just tell me, 'Go to it!'
But nobody asks whether I *want* to do it.
I wonder if they'd think that things were so fine
If they had to do headstands at parties of mine!"

Elizabeth grew to be nine or ten,
And she took up the clarinet and then
When her parents had parties for people they'd met,
After dinner, they'd make Lizzie play clarinet.
Night after night, they'd have Liz entertain
And the truth is, for her, it was less fun than pain.
"It's strange," Lizzie thought. "They just tell me, 'Go to it!'
But nobody asks me if I *want* to do it."
And she said to herself, "Liz, do people like *you*?
Or do they only like all the things you can do?"

Then finally one evening when Liz was fourteen,
Her folks gave a party, the biggest she'd seen.
"All right!" yelled her dad, "May I have your attention?
You will now see a stunt almost too swell to mention.
Our Liz will do something you'll never forget—
She will stand on her head while playing Chopin on her clarinet!"
"On your mark," cried her mother. "Get set, girl, now go!"
The whole room grew quiet. And Lizzie said, ". . . No."
"No?" said her father. "Why what a strange word."
"She means yes," said her mother. "We must have misheard."
"No," replied Lizzie, "you heard what I said.
I will not play Chopin while I stand on my head."

"But why not?" said her mother. "Yes, why?" asked her dad.
Elizabeth's answer was simple and sad.
"It's always seemed strange. You just tell me, 'Go to it!'
But nobody cares whether I *want* to do it.
It makes me feel awful. I wish you'd explain
Why you only seem happy when I entertain.
There are things I can do and things I can be.
I know you like them. But do you like me?"

There was silence till softly her father said, "Oh . . ."
Then, "Oh . . ." said her mother. "We just didn't know."
"We're sorry," her dad said, "and we'll try to change."
"We love you," her mom said, "and it does seem strange
The way that we've always just told you, 'Go to it!'
Without ever asking if you *want* to do it."
So they sent all the party guests off on their way.
And they had a nice dinner . . .
Just the three of them . . .
Talking and listening . . .
And especially listening . . . to what Liz had to say.

In My Room

Words and Music by Bobby Gosh
Illustrated by Petra Mathers

♪ music on page 232

There's a place where I love to be
Far away from my family,
And it's near enough so I'm right close by their side.
There's a place I can call my own
When I'm sad and want to be alone,
Or when I'm happy or when I just need a place to hide.

In my room, in my room,
In my own very special room,
I can always find a place
To call my room.
It can be most anywhere,
Under a table or behind a chair,
And my favorite place to be
Is in my room.

Sometimes my mom or dad
Will make me a little mad,
Then I need a place to be with only me.
I'll make believe I'm a rock 'n' roll star
And maybe play a little air guitar
Or read awhile or maybe watch TV.

In my room, in my room,
In my own very special room,
I can be anyone I want to be
In my room.
I can do anything I dare
And pretend that I'm anywhere,
Yes, my favorite place to be
Is in my room.

Some people don't read the sign
That says this place is mine,
Please knock before you enter my own room.
Then I might say, "Come on in!
How're you doin'? Where've you been?
Make yourself at home here in my room!"

In my room, in my room,
In my own very special room,
I can be anyone I want to be
In my room.
I can do anything I dare
And pretend that I'm anywhere,
Yes, my favorite place to be
Is in my room.

My Grandma

by Letty Cottin Pogrebin
Illustrated by Susan Stillman

I used to be ashamed of my Grandma.

I know that's a terrible thing to say, but it was true until last Wednesday, so I have to admit it.

My Grandma lives in our basement.

She moved in about a year ago after Grandpa died. Mom and Dad put a Chinese screen in front of the water heater and stuck a blue rug on the floor, so it looks pretty nice for a basement. Grandma says she can be happy anywhere as long as she has a hard bed and her exercise bike.

My Grandma loves her exercise bike. She rides for twenty minutes every day and she's almost seventy. She makes me ride for ten minutes because she says I'm only half as strong as she is even if I'm sixty years younger.

"A sound mind needs a sound body," she says. But she talks funny so it comes out *a zound mind nids a zound body*.

My Grandma is from the Old Country. When I was little, I thought that was just a nice way of saying she was *old*, but it means she wasn't born here. She grew up speaking Yiddish and Polish and Hungarian and I forget what else, but whatever it was, it definitely makes her English sound weird. That's just *one* of the things I used to get embarrassed about.

At first I was glad she moved in because she's kind of fun to be with. She lets me braid her long gray hair, and she teaches me things like gin rummy and knitting and how to make those little pastries with nuts and sugar rolled up in them. She calls them *rugalach*. I can't say it as well as she does so I call them ruggies.

I used to love Grandma's stories, too.

No matter what we're doing, she always slaps her forehead and says "Oy, that reminds me of a story."

One time when we were baking, she remembered how she once churned butter so long it turned to cheese. "I was daytime dreaming," she said with a laugh.

And once we were sewing and my scissors wouldn't cut, and she told me about this guy who used to ride through the streets of her town with a special cart with a sharpener.

"He made a clang on his cowbell," she said, "and we ran out from our houses with our dull knives and scissors, and he sharpened them on a big stone wheel. Such sparks you never saw."

I told her that sounded pretty neat. I wish we had one of those guys in our neighborhood.

When there's a full moon outside, my Grandma always pulls down the window shades near my bed. She says it's bad luck if the moon shines on you when you sleep. I make fun of her superstitions but she always says, "You never know . . . you never know."

Mostly, my Grandma's stories are funny. But sometimes they're scary—so scary that I have to scrunch up my shoulders to cover my ears, even if I've heard them before.

For instance, there's the one about her aunt and uncle who lived in this poor little town with a winding brook and a wooden bridge. It sounds like she's starting a fairy tale but I know she's working up to the part about the pogroms. That's when these soldiers called Cossacks attacked and burned Jewish people's houses. We're Jewish.

"If it wasn't for the pogroms," she says, "a lot of Jews who ran away to America would have stayed in Europe. Then they would have been killed by the Nazis. So maybe the pogroms were a blessing in disguise."

To me that's like saying, "Good thing we were hit by a two-ton bus or we might've been flattened by a ten-ton truck."

But to Grandma it's a happy ending. Grandma *loves* happy endings.

The trouble started when my friend Katy found Grandma's false teeth floating in a glass on the bathroom sink. I guess I was so used to seeing them that I didn't even notice them anymore. But Katy noticed. She shouted, "Yuuuck! Gross!" and started laughing hysterically, and pretending to talk to them and making them talk back. I had to get down on my knees and *beg* her to shut up so my grandmother wouldn't hear and get her feelings hurt.

After that happened, I started to realize there were a *million* things about Grandma that were embarrassing. Like the way she grabs my face in her palms and murmurs "*Shaine maidel*" which means "beautiful girl" in Yiddish. What would Katy say if she saw *that*!

Or how Grandma always says her *B'rachas* before she eats. *B'rachas* are Hebrew blessings that thank God for things. All I can say is my Grandma must really be hungry because what she eats isn't exactly worth a thank-you note. Chopped herring is gross enough but white bread soaking in warm milk could make a regular person throw up.

And that's just the problem. My friends are regular people. So when Katy or Jill or Angie are around, I have to worry about what Grandma's going to do next.

Once she took me and Jill out to Burger King, even though she doesn't eat there herself because they don't have kosher meat. Instead of ordering our hamburgers well done, she told the person behind the counter "They'll have two Whoppers well-to-do." Jill burst out laughing, but I almost died.

Another thing I spend half my life explaining is why my Grandma wears a wig. It's not a designer wig either. It's like the hair on an old doll, sort of frizzy and brownish.

I have to explain that she doesn't wear it because her hair fell out and she doesn't wear it to change her hairdo. She wears it because the Jewish law she believes in says that after a woman gets married, she's not allowed to show her own hair to anyone but her husband.

"But he died," Katy said. "So what does he care now?"

Some things you just can't explain.

After a while, I started wishing I could hide my Grandma in a closet. It got so bad I even complained to my parents.

"You guys are at work all afternoon! You don't know what it's *like*. She barges in and talks nonstop. She tries to teach us thousand-year-old games that aren't even in English. And she looks like the Grandmother From Another Planet."

My parents said they understood how I felt, but I had to be careful not to make Grandma feel unwelcome in our house.

"She's had a very tough life," said my Dad.

"Try to make the best of it," said my Mom.

I was trying, *believe* me, I was trying.

Then, like I told you, on Wednesday, something happened that changed everything. My teacher made an announcement that our school was going to be a part of a big Oral History Project. We were supposed to help find interesting old people and interview them about their lives so kids in the future will understand how things used to be.

I was trying to think if I knew anyone interesting when Angie nudged me from across the aisle.

"Volunteer your grandmother!" she whispered.

I was shocked.

"My Grandma??" I said.

"Yeah!" Angie said. "*She's* interesting!"

Interesting? That's the *last* thing I ever thought Angie would say about Grandma!

Well, okay, I said to myself. Why not? Talking is what my Grandma likes to do best. In fact, I've never been able to get her to stop.

So that's how I ended up here. The whole school is in the auditorium for a big assembly and I'm up here on the stage interviewing my own Grandma.

We have microphones clipped to our shirts and TV cameras pointed at us and a bunch of professors are standing off to the side in case I need help asking questions.

Which I don't.

After all this time, nobody knows my Grandma's stories better than I do. I just say the right thing to get her started.

Like when I say "Grandma, why did you leave the Old Country?" she goes right into how the Nazis took over her town.

I've heard all that before. But then she starts telling this incredible story that is brand new to me:

"My parents, they sold all their furniture to buy passage to America. In the meantime, they hid me in a broken-down barn under a pile of straw.

"Can you believe it?" Grandma says looking right at me. "When I was only a little older than you are now, I was running from the Nazis. Me and my parents and my grandparents got into a big old ship, and people were getting sick during the trip and some of them even died. But we had a happy ending when we saw the Statue of Liberty."

While my Grandma talks, I see all my friends and teachers are listening to her as if she's a great hero. And suddenly I feel so proud of my Grandma, I could burst.

I can hardly wait to ask her the next question.

"How did it feel when you saw the Statue of Liberty, Grandma?"

"Very nice," she says. "When that lady she held up her lamp for us to come in nice and safe, I *knew* everything would be okay. I *knew* it."

Next she talks about her life in America and I hear her saying something else that she never put in any of her stories before. She's telling us that she loved her family very much, but she has to admit one thing: that she used to be ashamed of her grandmother.

"For twenty years that woman was in this country, but she wouldn't learn English never," says my Grandma about her Grandma. "Such a shame she was to me in front of my American girlfriends."

I can't believe my ears. I feel a little stabbing pain in my heart. And right there on the stage I make a *B'racha* to thank God for never letting my Grandma know I was ashamed of her, too.

"Thank you for sharing your experiences—the happy ones and the painful ones," the principal is saying to Grandma. "We're so glad your granddaughter brought you to us today."

Everyone starts clapping really loud. I feel like laughing and crying at the same time. I feel like hugging my Grandma and saying I'm sorry and nominating her for the Grammy Award for Grandmothers.

But I just stand on the stage and listen to the applause, and I feel my Grandma grip my hand tight as we take our bows together.

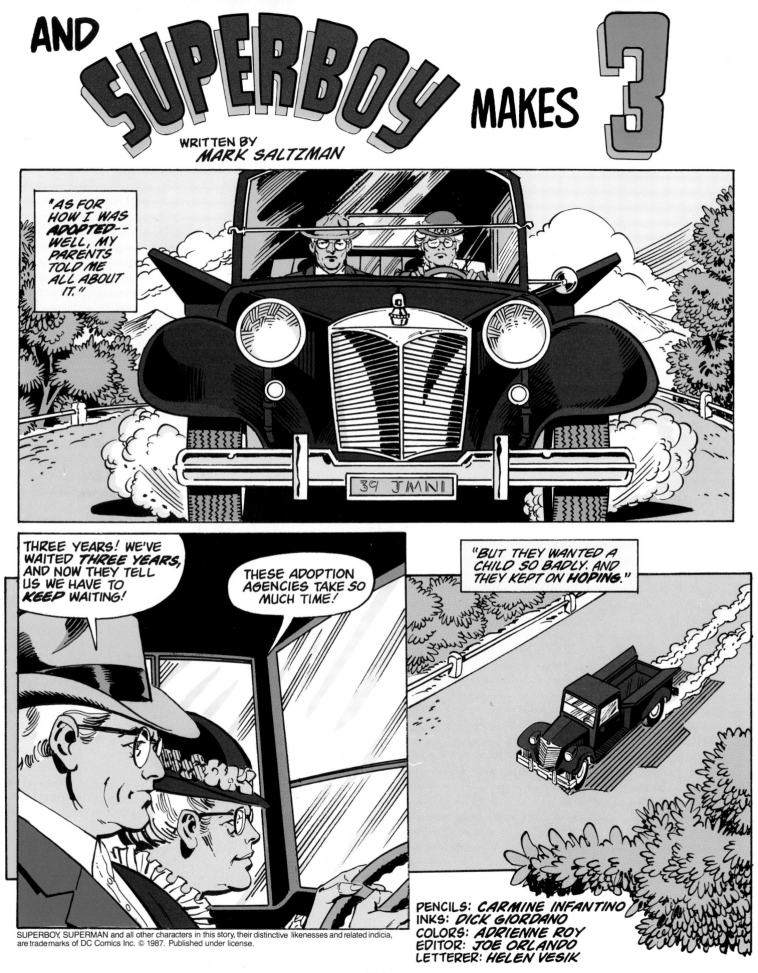

AND *SUPERBOY* MAKES 3

WRITTEN BY **MARK SALTZMAN**

"AS FOR HOW I WAS *ADOPTED*-- WELL, MY PARENTS TOLD ME ALL ABOUT IT."

THREE YEARS! WE'VE WAITED *THREE YEARS,* AND NOW THEY TELL US WE HAVE TO *KEEP* WAITING!

THESE ADOPTION AGENCIES TAKE *SO* MUCH TIME!

"BUT THEY WANTED A CHILD SO BADLY. AND THEY KEPT ON *HOPING.*"

PENCILS: *CARMINE INFANTINO*
INKS: *DICK GIORDANO*
COLORS: *ADRIENNE ROY*
EDITOR: *JOE ORLANDO*
LETTERER: *HELEN VESIK*

I GUESS WE'VE JUST GOT TO BE *PATIENT*, MARTHA. AFTER ALL...

SCREEECH!

JONATHAN, YOU'RE JUST NOT GOING TO *BELIEVE* THIS!

2

I'm Never Afraid

Words and Music by
Sarah Durkee and Christopher Cerf
Illustrated by Hilary Knight

♪ music on page 233

Sometimes I'm afraid of what would happen to me
   if someone came and took me away.
And sometimes I'm afraid of stuff that's on TV,
   or worried if my mom's okay.
And sometimes I'm so scared about the monsters in my closet
   I hardly even dare to blink.
But one thing I can tell you you should never be afraid of
   is sayin' what you really think!

Oh, no, I'm never afraid, I'm never afraid
   to say what's on my mind!
No, I'm never afraid, I'm never afraid
   to say what's on my mind!
There's all kinds of brave
   and all kinds of courageous,
But me I'm the bravest kind,
   'cause I'm never afraid to say what's on my mind!

Well Annie's scared of heights and Dan's afraid of snakes
   and I'm scared to pass the bully next door.
And sometimes I'm afraid they'll make a stupid mistake
   and someone'll start a nuclear war!
But once this kid was braggin' 'bout a brand new bike
   he was plannin' to go out and steal.
I said, "It's *dumb* to do that!" and I wasn't afraid
   'cause I told him how I really feel!

(To Say What's on My Mind)

Oh, no, I'm never afraid, I'm never afraid
    to say what's on my mind!
No, I'm never afraid, I'm never afraid
    to say what's on my mind!
There's all kinds of brave
    and all kinds of courageous,
But me I'm the bravest kind,
    'cause I'm never afraid to say what's on my mind!

I know a macho guy who pumps his muscles every day
Who's *ter-ri-fied* of sayin' somethin' wrong!
I know a little boy who says the hardest things to say,
Yeah, *he's the one* who's really big and strong!

My mother's got a friend who likes to hug me a lot,
    yeah, he's nice to me beyond a doubt.
But if somebody hugs me and it bugs me a lot,
    I say "Mom, they've gotta CUT THAT OUT!"
You might be scared the truth is gonna make 'em mad,
    and you're petrified to have a fight,
But come right out and say it and you won't be afraid,
    if you're sayin' what you know is right!

Oh, no, I'm never afraid, I'm never afraid
    to say what's on my mind!
No, I'm never afraid, I'm never afraid
    to say what's on my mind!
There's all kinds of brave
    and all kinds of courageous,
But me I'm the bravest kind,
    'cause I'm never afraid to say what's on my mind!

121

Two Can Play the Same Game

by Mavis Jukes
Illustrated by Pierre Le-Tan

Maria was holding a rubber pig wrapped up in a dish towel.

"What have you got there?" said her grandfather.

"An alive pig," said Maria. She slyly reached inside the towel and squeezed the squeaker.

The pig oinked.

Her grandfather put his crossword puzzle and his pencil on the coffee table. "Well, let's have a look," he said.

Maria walked over. Her grandfather lifted a corner of the towel and slowly shook his head, and whistled. "That's one nice-looking hog," he said to Maria.

"Thank you," said Maria.

Her grandfather's stomach growled. "But I'll tell you something—he's hungry."

Maria stared at the pig.

"Give him to me—I'll hold him," said her grandfather. "And you go warm him up a tortilla and throw in some of that cold chicken in the refrigerator."

"And that leftover guacamole!" he added, as Maria left the room.

Maria warmed a tortilla, rolled up some chicken and guacamole inside it, and brought it into the living room.

"Where's the milk?" said her grandfather.

"WHAT milk?" said Maria.

"Didn't I say this pig needs milk?"

"No," said Maria. "Nobody said anything about milk."

"The pig needs milk," said her grandfather.

Maria loudly sighed. She went into the kitchen and poured milk into a red plastic cup.

When she returned, the tortilla was gone.

"Boy," said her grandfather, wiping his moustache. "That was one hungry pig."

Maria said nothing. She put the cup of milk on the coffee table.

"No pig should ever get that hungry. Or this cold!" said her grandfather. "Feel this hoof. Feel it!"

Maria felt the pig's hoof.

"The pig is fine," she said.

"Fine?" said her grandfather. "FINE? This pig's so cold it makes me cold to look at him."

"The pig is not cold," said Maria. "The pig is wrapped up in a blanket."

"The pig is wrapped up in a dish towel," said her grandfather. He held the pig closer to his chest. *"Pobrecito,"* he said in a soft voice. "Poor little thing."

Maria stormed out of the room. She returned, dragging a striped blanket with fringe on the ends. She picked up the plastic cup and peered into it; it was empty.

"Very thirsty, that pig," said Maria's grandfather, taking the blanket from Maria and pulling it over his knees.

Maria stared at her grandfather as he cradled the pig on one arm and drew the blanket up under its snout.

He bent his head over the pig. "Hey, little *bandido*," he said in a sweet voice. "Is your belly full?" He tickled the top of the pig's head and gave the pig a kiss.

Maria frowned at the pig.

"Yes," said her grandfather. "I've got to congratulate you, Maria. You've got yourself one handsome animal, and I should know. You know how many pigs I've raised in my day?"

"No," said Maria.

"Many pigs. And I'll tell you something: a pig is a very sensitive and intelligent animal. I knew a pig that could smoke a pipe."

"You did not," said Maria.

"Oh, yes I did!" said her grandfather. "The pig could smoke a pipe and watch TV. Of course, not everybody can teach a pig to smoke a pipe—and not every pig can learn. But, hand me my pipe, will you?" he said to Maria. "And my tobacco. I'll see what I can do. And turn on the TV, while you're up."

Maria tromped across the rug and turned on the TV and brought her grandfather his pipe and tobacco.

He handed her the pig. "See if he'll watch TV while I get this ready," he said.

Maria sat down beside her grandfather on the arm of his chair while he packed his pipe. She unwrapped the pig and let it stand on her lap.

She watched cowboys galloping across the screen, watched cowboys drink whiskey and argue about a poker game. "The pig doesn't want cowboys," said Maria. "The pig wants *Wild World of Animals.*"

Her grandfather sighed. "But this is John Wayne!"

"I can't help that," said Maria. "The pig is very intelligent—he wants *Wild World of Animals.*"

Her grandfather looked over at her.

"He does!" said Maria.

"I just got comfortable," said her grandfather.

Maria said nothing. She stared at the screen. Now the cowboys were sitting around a campfire. Suddenly she covered the pig's eyes with her hand. "Don't look!" she cried.

She turned to her grandfather. "They're frying bacon!" she whispered. "He's very sensitive! Change the channel!"

With a grunt, Maria's grandfather got up and slowly walked across the room. He stood in front of the TV for a moment, before turning the knob.

Maria quickly slid from the arm of the chair onto the cushion and kicked off her shoes and covered herself and the pig with the blanket.

"And the pig wants popcorn," said Maria.

A Father Like That

by Charlotte Zolotow
Illustrated by Petra Mathers

I wish I had a father.
But my father went away
before I was born.
I say to my mother,
You know what he'd be like?
"What?" she says.

If he were here,
we'd leave the house together every day.

We'd walk to the corner
together.
And he'd go left to work.
And I'd go right to school.
So long, old man,
till tonight, he'd say.

When he'd come home at night, I'd meet him at the door.
He'd put his arm around me and say,
We made another day, the two of us,
and we'd both laugh.

He'd make a drink for you and a drink for him,
and he'd make you sit down
with him before dinner.

After dinner, we'd all do the dishes together
instead of just you and me,
and I'd do my homework.
When I got stuck, he'd show me how.

And pretty soon he'd say,
Hurry up so we can play
a game of checkers before bedtime.

But at bedtime
he'd say to you,
Oh, just one more.

When I'd be sick in bed,
he'd bring me home a new book
and tell you to lie down
while he sat with me and cheered me up.

He'd bring home good jokes from the office
and say, Hey, old fellow,
have you heard this?
And I'd tell it to all the kids the next day.

He'd rather go down to the store
and have a Coke with me
than sit around having beer
with some other fathers.
He'd never call me sissy if I cried.
He'd just say, Never mind, old fellow,
you'll feel better later on.

He would come in the night
when I had nightmares
and talk to me.

He'd never show off about what a good father he was
at parent-teacher meetings.
And if Miss Barton told him I talk in class,
he'd say, Why sure, all boys do.

And no matter what happened,
he'd be on my side when things went wrong,
even if sometimes he had to say
it was really my fault.

When something bad happened,
I could always
talk to him.

His voice would be very low,
and when he was angry,
He would speak slowly and be kind.

He'd know all my friends by name
and ask something sensible like,
How's your dog?

He'd never joke about me to my friends
or say, Break it up, boys,
to send them home.

He'd understand why
I don't want to wear
that green shirt,
and he'd say to you,
You never were a boy.
You don't know.

He would wrestle with me, and when I wanted
he wouldn't mind if I pounced him a bit.
We'd listen to the doubleheaders together on TV.
When you'd say, Turn it down,
He'd smile and say,
If we make it lower, we won't hear.

And all the while
I'm telling this to my mother,
she is sewing very fast.
"I'll tell you what,"
she says, when I stop talking,
"I like the kind of father
you're talking about.
And in case he never comes,
just remember

when you grow up,
you can be
a father like that yourself!"

The Day Dad Made Toast

by Sarah Durkee
Illustrated by Richard McNeel

I'll never forget the day Dad made toast. It was a sunny Saturday morning in late October near Halloween. I remember it was Halloween because Mom was outside putting a scarecrow with a pumpkin head up on the roof. Dad was in bed.

"Hey kids!" he hollered from their bedroom. "C'mere!"

My older sister Lucy and little brother Danny and I were busy watching the Three Stooges, but we ran upstairs during the commercial. Dad sprang out of bed in his underwear like a ringmaster.

"Here they are!" he bellowed joyfully. "My *kids!!* The greatest kids in the *world!*" He grabbed us to his chest and squished our faces together. This wasn't at all like him. Something was up. "Where's your beautiful mother?!"

"Out on the roof," Lucy said.

He pulled us over to the window that looked out onto the roof. My mom was out there in her ripped overalls with a bunch of tools sticking out of her pockets. She had finished setting up the pumpkin man and was now fixing the TV antenna. Dad tapped on the window.

"LINDA!" he shouted. "COME ON IN, HONEY!"

Mom looked up cheerfully. She had nails in her mouth.

"JUSHT A SHECUND!" she yelled. "I SHEE A LOOSH SHINGLE!"

Clutching her hammer, she scrambled toward the shingle on all fours.

Dad grinned down at us.

"Should I tell her?" he asked.

Mom's hammering rang through the house.

"Tell her *what??* What's going *on??*"

"Well . . ." Dad smiled, and then he broke the big news. "I'M GOING TO MAKE TOAST!!"

"WOW!" we cried. "*Really,* Dad?? *Today??*"

"Yup!" he beamed proudly. "Right this minute! And we're not talking ordinary ho-hum *toast,* believe you me . . . we're talking dad's special *cinnamon* toast!! And I don't want your mom to lift a *finger,* I'm handling the *whole thing!*"

"Oooooh!"

He tapped on the window again. "LINDA!" he yelled. "MEET US IN THE KITCHEN! I HAVE A SURPRISE FOR YOU!"

131

"OKAY, SWEETHEART!" Mom shouted as she hung from a ladder, clearing leaves from the gutter. "I'LL BE RIGHT DOWN!"

Lucy and Danny and I sat on the end of the bed, waiting for further instructions. We love it when he gets in these moods. One time he decided we should cook Thanksgiving dinner on the outdoor grill. It tasted weird. Another time he decided the whole family was getting flabby, and we started doing calisthenics out in the yard every morning. On the third day he twisted his ankle, so we stopped.

Dad went over to the chair where he always throws his clothes at night and pulled on his jeans. "Okay, kids, listen up!" he said. "Your mother and I both work really hard all week. I figure the least I can do . . ."

Mom started hammering something again.

"I FIGURE THE LEAST I CAN DO," he shouted over the banging, "IS TAKE SOME OF THE HOUSEWORK LOAD OFF HER ONCE IN A WHILE! WE'VE ALL GOT TO LEND A HAND! PITCH IN! DO OUR BIT! SHE'LL REALLY APPRECIATE IT!"

The hammering stopped. Dad pulled on a T-shirt that says "Are we having fun yet?" and jabbed his fist in the air like a football coach.

"Let's hit that kitchen, team!"

We raced him downstairs.

The kitchen was still pretty neat from the night before. We all kind of wandered around for a second not quite knowing how to start. Dad opened and closed a few cabinets. "Now let's see . . ." he muttered. "*Plates.* . . . Where do we keep the ones I like . . . y'know those big blue plates we have? . . ."

Mom knocked on the kitchen door with her elbow. She was lugging two pots of geraniums. Dad flung open the door and gave her a kiss.

"Thanks!" Mom said as she passed through to the living room. "It's about time I brought these indoors!"

Dad sort of jogged along behind her to the doorway. "Breakfast is coming right up, angelface! I'm making my special *cinnamon* toast! Just leave everything to me! You're gonna *love* it!"

Mom's voice drifted back from the family room. "Terrific, hon!"

"Um . . . Linda?" he called. "Where are the big blue plates?"

"In the dishwasher!" Mom yelled.

Dad snapped his fingers. "RIGHT!"

Danny and I got the plates and juice glasses from the dishwasher and started to put them on the table. Mom came back in dragging the vacuum cleaner behind her. She picked up the phone and called her office.

"No, no, kids!" said Dad. "The plates have to be *preheated!* That's what they do in fancy restaurants. It makes the toast stay warm longer!" He grabbed the plates, put them in the oven, and turned away.

"Oh," we said. We turned the oven on. Dad's very absent-minded.

"Hi, it's me," Mom said on the phone. "I spoke to the Blums and they're willing to go to seventy-three-five. They'd like to pass papers on Thursday."

Mom's a real estate agent. They all talk like that.

She hung up the phone, plugged in the vacuum, and rounded the corner to the dining room accompanied by a whir so deafening that we all had to shout.

"OKAY," Dad yelled, "LET'S GET THIS SHOW ON THE ROAD! JENNY,"—that's me—"WE NEED ABOUT A DOZEN SLICES OF BREAD! *WHITE* BREAD, NOT THE HEALTHY KIND."

"BUT MOM LIKES US TO USE THE HEALTHY KIND!" I reminded him.

"JUST THIS *ONCE!* THIS IS 'DAD'S SPECIAL TOAST'! HEALTHY BREAD DOESN'T WORK! NOW WHERE'S THAT DARN TOASTER?!"

"HERE, DAD!" Danny giggled. It had a quilted toaster cover over it.

"WHY WOULD ANYBODY WANT TO COVER UP A TOASTER?!" Dad grumbled.

Lucy and I tried not to laugh but Danny was too young to know any better.

"DADDY COULDN'T FIND THE *TOASTER!*" he shrieked. "HEEE HEE HEE HA HA HA!!"

"I *KNOW* WHERE THE *TOASTER* IS, DANNY, I JUST COULDN'T *SEE* IT! NOW GET OVER THERE AND HELP JENNY COUNT THE BREAD."

The vacuuming stopped. Mom walked through on her way down to the laundry room with a huge armload of dirty clothes.

"Uh, Linda?" Dad said brightly with his head in a cupboard. "Sugar?"

"Yes, cupcake?" she answered.

"No, honey, I mean *where's the sugar,*" said Dad. "I don't see it in here."

"Bottom shelf!" yelled Mom on her way to the basement.

"RIGHT!" yelled Dad, spotting the sugar bag. "Okay, kids! Start toasting that bread! Lucy, you and I will make the cinnamon mixture. Let's see . . . cinnamon . . . sugar . . ."

"How about a bowl to mix it in?" said Lucy, handing him a bowl.

"RIGHT!" said Dad. "Now watch closely." He started spooning sugar and shaking cinnamon. "*Equal parts* of each. That's the real secret to this. A lot of people skimp on the cinnamon."

Mom started a buzz saw in the basement. She's been building new shelves for the family room. Also a sun deck. Also an addition to the garage.

"How's that first batch of toast coming, guys?" Dad called to Danny and me.

"Okay," I said. "What should we do when it's done?"

Mom came up from the basement tugging a bag of cement mix. "Bulkhead's stuck shut," she said. "I better go out and pry it open."

"Butter it and bring it over to me and Lucy *fast,*" Dad said. "We'll sprinkle it with the cinnamon mixture and then whisk each batch into the oven with the preheated plates."

Mom muscled the cement mix out the kitchen door.

"There's orange juice in the fridge," she called over her shoulder.

"Don't you budge, sweetie!" Dad called after her. "I'll take care of it!"

Danny poured the juice and put napkins on the table. I kept buttering the toast when it popped up and IMMEDIATELY brought it to Dad who IMMEDIATELY sprinkled it with the cinnamon mixture and gave it to Lucy who IMMEDIATELY put it in the oven with the preheated plates. Once we'd gotten our system down pat, Dad relaxed a little.

"Y'know, kids," he mused, "times have really changed. I mean *my* father wouldn't have been caught *dead* doing any housework. It just wasn't something men *did;* it was women's work. But we're modern families now, and here you have a manly guy like me pitching in like this after a hard week's work—making breakfast so his wife can take a little break. It's beautiful, isn't it?"

"It's beautiful, Dad."

"We've really come a long way," he said.

"We really have, Dad."

Just as Lucy was putting the last piece of toast in the oven, Mom knocked on the door with her elbow again. "COULD SOMEBODY OPEN THE DOOR, PLEASE?"

Dad rushed over to let her in.

"Thanks. My hands are *filthy!* I didn't even want to touch the doorknob!"

"Ready for the most delicious toast you've ever had in your life, Linda?!" said Dad. We all gathered around the oven.

"Can I wash my hands first?" said Mom. "Or is the flavor peaking this very *second*?"

"Linda, this is no time for sarcasm. Just wash your hands and sit down and relax," said Dad, "and I'll serve you! You too, kids."

Mom washed her hands at the sink, and Lucy, Danny, and I sat down at the table.

"I poured the juice," said Danny.

"You did a great job," Mom smiled as she joined us. "No spills."

"O-kee do-kee!" sang Dad as he opened the oven and brought out the plates. "Hot plates for everybody! Dad's special method!"

He set one in front of each of us.

"Thanks, honey," Mom said.

"Thanks, Dad!!" we all chimed. It did feel like a special occasion. A party, almost, the way he did it.

"And now . . . the *pièce de résistance!* My crowning achievement! The main event! Ladies and gentlemen . . . DAD'S SPECIAL TOAST!!!"

He set the big plate of warm, crispy, buttery cinnamon toast in the center of the table.

"YAAAAAAAAY!!" we all cheered. "Hooray for Daaaaaaad!!" we applauded.

Dad took a bow and sat down to eat.

Everybody took a couple of pieces of toast and started ooohing and ahhing like mad.

"UNBELIEVABLE!" said Lucy. "The best I've ever had! By far!"

"FRIGHTENINGLY good," said Mom. "Beyond toast. Indescribably delicious."

"Extraterrestrial," I said. "Yummy in the tummy."

We all munched in silence for a minute.

Then Danny spoke up.

"What's the big deal?" said Danny. "All he did was make toast."

"Danny!" Lucy scolded. "That's not very nice! It's really *great* toast!"

"*Perfect* toast!" I cried.

"*Warm* toast!" Mom added.

We all went back to munching.

"But Mom does a million times more housework every *day,* and we hardly even thank her at all! And we NEVER go 'Yaaaay.' "

We all looked at Danny.

Then we looked at Mom.

Everybody was quiet.

Then Dad took a deep breath.

He started yelling "YAAAAAAAAY!" at the top of his lungs, and then so did Lucy and Danny and I, and we made Mom get up and take a bow.

"Thank you!" she laughed, pretending she was holding a microphone. "You're a beautiful audience! It's a pleasure to be here!"

We whistled and hollered and clapped and stamped our feet.

Mom blew a kiss like a movie star and raised her glass of orange juice.

"A toast!" she declared.

"A toast!" said Lucy, lifting her glass.

"A toast!" said Dad, holding up a piece of toast.

"To my perfect, helpful children," said Mom.

"Yeah!" we said.

"To my loving, supportive husband," said Mom.

"Hear, hear!" Dad said.

"To the yard!" said Mom. She put down her glass and grinned.

"Huh?" we said.

"To the *yard*," Mom repeated, gesturing toward the pile of cement bags. "What do you say we go work off some of that hearty breakfast?"

She headed for the door, then turned and winked. "Oh, and by the way . . . what are you guys making for dinner?"

(P.S. . . . We went out for pizza.)

The Stupid Song

Words and Music by Robin Batteau
Illustrated by Gary Zamchick

♪ music on page 234

BROTHER
Everything's so stupid, stupid, stupid, stupid, stupid, stupid, stupid,
And I hate it, hate it, hate it, hate it, hate it, hate it,
Maybe if I say it, say it, say it, say it, say it to myself,
I won't have to yell at my mom.

Bein' a kid is no bowl of cherries,
No bed of roses,
No piece of cake.
When I act like a grown-up,
They say I'm precocious.
When I act like a kid,
They tell me that I'm hopeless.

SISTER
Everything's so stupid, stupid, stupid, stupid, stupid, stupid, stupid,
And I hate it, hate it, hate it, hate it, hate it, hate it,
Maybe if I say it, say it, say it, say it, say it to myself,
I won't have to yell at my dad.

Bein' a kid is no laughing matter,
No silver platter,
No yellow brick road.
When I say what I think,
They say, "Kid, you're too young."
And then when I'm quiet,
They say, "Cat got your tongue?"

MOM AND DAD (in unison)
Everything's so stupid, stupid, stupid, stupid, stupid, stupid, stupid,
And we hate it, hate it, hate it, hate it, hate it, hate it,
Maybe if we say it, say it, say it, say it, say it to ourselves,
We won't have to yell at our kids.

Bein' a grown-up's no spring picnic,
No day at the beach,
No easy street.
Even if you're makin'
   their favorite treat,
You can lead your kids to lunch
But you can't make 'em eat!

THE FAMILY
Everything's so stupid, stupid, stupid, stupid, stupid, stupid, stupid,
And I hate it, hate, it hate it, hate it, hate it, hate it,
Maybe if I say it, say it, say it, say it, say it to myself,
I won't have to yell at . . . THEM!

Jimmy Says

Words by David Buskin and Abra Bigham,
Music by David Buskin
Illustrated by Artie Ruiz

♪ music on page 231

BIG BROTHER: Hey, kid, you're lookin' pretty down in the dumps. Tell your big brother about it.

LITTLE BROTHER: Aw, it's just the kids at school. They keep tellin' me what I *should* do, and what I *shouldn't* do, and I'm afraid if I don't listen to them, well, they might not want to be my friends anymore.

BIG BROTHER: Hey, don't worry. There's a guy in my class that used to make *me* feel that way all the time, too. And then one day, I figured out there's another way to go. . . .

Jimmy says, "Do this . . ."
Jimmy says, "Do this . . ."
I say, "I don't want to!"
Jimmy says, "Do this . . ."
Jimmy says, "Do this . . ."
I say, "I don't want to!"

Trying to make up my own mind,
Got my own direction to find!
Yeah, I know Jimmy's cool,
And everyone in school
Usually does what Jimmy does
Without thinking, just because

Jimmy says, "Try this . . ."
Jimmy says, "Try this . . ."
I say, "I don't need it!"
Jimmy says, "Try this . . .
Come on and try this!"
I say, "I don't think I need it!"

Sometimes it's just no fun
To feel like you're the only one
Who doesn't go along
When something seems wrong.
But they're not my friends if they can't see
I don't like people pushing me!

"Hey, what's the matter with you?"
"Come on, man! Everybody's going!"
"Chicken!"
"Nobody'll ever know."
"What are you, scared?"
"Everybody does it."

I might hang out with Jim,
But I don't need to be just like him.
Got to listen to myself,
'Cause you can't let someone else
Always make your move for you!
Got to find out what *you* want to do!

140

The Night We Started Dancing

by Ann Cameron
Illustrated by Eve Chwast

I am named after my dad, Luis, but everybody calls me Luisito. I live with my grandfather and grandmother; my four uncles; my two aunts; my cousin, Diego; a girl named Maria who helps my grandmother; our two dogs, Chubby and Pilot; our two cats, Stripes and Hunter; and our big green parrot, Bright Star, that my grandmother always says she is going to bake and serve for dinner someday.

We live in a town called Santa Cruz, in Guatemala, Central America. Santa Cruz has a park where there are great band concerts, free, every week. It has a public school, and a big college for army cadets, and it has an electronics store where you could special-order a computer, but it doesn't have paved streets, it has only dirt streets that turn to dust in the winter when it's dry, and to mud in the summer when it rains.

I like dirt streets. It goes with the special thing about Santa Cruz, which is that it's a very old town. It was a town before Columbus discovered America, and before the Spaniards came from Spain to steal our land and our gold and make slaves of people, because they said their religion was the true one, and God liked them better than us.

On the edge of Santa Cruz there is a high hill covered with old pine trees and the ruins of pyramids and an ancient fortress. That's where the headquarters of our people was, the headquarters of the kingdom of the Quichés,* where our ancestors fought the Spaniards harder than anybody in Guatemala, before they lost for good.

Once, when I was six, a real Spaniard from Spain came to our house for dinner. He was going to do some business with my grandfather, so my grandmother invited him.

The whole dinner I kept watching my grandfather and the Spaniard all the time, and looking at my grandfather's big machete knife that he keeps by the front door.

Finally, I couldn't stand it. I said, "*Con permiso,* excuse me," and got up from the table and followed my grandmother into the kitchen when she went to get more food, and I even ducked under Bright Star's perch to get there faster.

*(pronounced kee-CHAYS)

"When?" I asked my grandmother. "When is he going to do it?"

"Who?" my grandmother said. "Do what?"

"When is Grandpa going to kill the Spaniard?" I whispered, and Bright Star hissed in his loudest voice, "Kill the Spaniard!" and the Spaniard looked around fast and dropped his fork.

My grandfather stopped munching his tortilla. "Don't be concerned," he said to the Spaniard, "we just have a crazy parrot," and my grandmother said, "One day I am going to bake you, Bright Star!"

Then she took me into one of the bedrooms and closed the door.

"What is this all about?" she said. "Why would Grandpa kill the Spaniard?"

"For being a Spaniard," I said.

"Are you crazy?" my grandmother said. "How can the Spaniard help being a Spaniard? He was born one, just like you were born a Guatemalan and a Quiché. Don't you know the battles with the Spaniards were over hundreds of years ago? We have to judge people by what they do, not by where they come from. And we have to fight our own battles, too, not the ones our ancestors fought."

So that was when I first found out that we'd never get our kingdom back—at least not the way it used to be.

My grandfather was born poor, and he never went to school. He worked from the time he was six years old, out in the wheat fields and the cornfields, hoeing. Every day when he finished work and went home, he would pass by his own dad in the street, drinking and spending all the family money. My great-granddad never helped my granddad at all. But my granddad just kept working, and when he was twenty, he started buying land—pieces nobody thought were good for anything—and on the land he planted apple orchards, and when the apples grew all over, big and beautiful, he got rich. He built a big house for my grandmother and our family, with five big bedrooms, and a patio in the middle full of flowers, and a living room where he and my grandmother put up all the pictures of both their families, except my grandfather never put up a picture of his dad. Then, last year, he must have finally started feeling sorry for his father, because he got his picture out of a drawer, and dusted it off, and put it up in the living room, only not with the rest of the pictures. So now my great-grandfather is staring out at the rest of the family, kind of ashamed-looking, from behind a fern.

My grandmother only learned to read four years ago, but she made my aunts and uncles study hard in school, and now she's making me do it, too. When I asked her why I had to study so hard, she said, "So that you aren't working with a hoe in the fields all your life, with the sun beating down on your head like a hammer."

When my grandparents' kids got to be old enough to study in the capital, my grandparents bought a house there for them to live in. So most of the year my aunts and uncles are there, studying architecture, and economics, and dentistry, and law, and accounting, and psychology. Only my youngest aunt, Celia, who is sixteen, is still living in Santa Cruz all the time. But next year she's going to the capital, too. She says she's going to study to be a doctor. My grandparents are very proud of all their children. The sad thing is, their oldest son, the only one who was studying agriculture and who loved the land the way my grandfather does, was my father, and he died. My mother died with him.

My mother was teaching grade school and my dad was in the last year of his agriculture studies when they died. I was four years old.

It happened four years ago, when my mom and dad and I and Uncle Ricardo were taking a bus from the capital to go back to my grandparents' house for Christmas. The bus terminal was full of dust and people trying to sell ice cream and coconuts and last-minute Christmas presents. Lots of people were going back to their hometowns for the holidays, and there weren't enough buses. Everybody was pushing and shoving to get on the ones there were.

My mom had a suitcase, and my dad had me on his back because he figured I couldn't run fast enough, and Uncle Ricardo was staring toward the sun with his hand shading his eyes, trying to see the bus that goes to Santa Cruz.

"Santa Cruz! That's it! Run!" he shouted, and my mom and dad raced for the front door of the bus, and Uncle Ricardo raced for the back, and they did flying dives over the top of a bunch of other people. My mom and dad got seats right behind the driver, and I sat on my mom's lap. Uncle Ricardo got stuck at the back, standing up.

Everybody pushed the windows down to get more air, and the driver put the bus in gear, but it didn't move, and his helper, the ticket taker, got out a hammer and a wrench and raised the hood on the bus and hammered on something for a while, and then the driver tried to move the bus again, and it went, and Uncle Ricardo heard my mother say, "A miracle! What a miraculous miracle!" and the ticket taker ran after the moving bus and jumped in the open door with the hammer and the wrench in his hand, and we were off.

Uncle Ricardo settled in and tried to take his elbow out of the stomach of the person on his right, and get his feet out from under the feet of the person on his left. My mom and dad were probably about the only ones who could see out the window, and who knew how the driver was driving.

The bus didn't go very fast, because it couldn't with so many people on it, but after a while Uncle Ricardo felt the bus lurch, and he heard my dad say to the driver, "Be careful, brother!" so he figured that the bus driver must have been taking a chance passing on a mountain curve.

A little while later he felt the bus twist again, and he heard my father say to the driver, "A man who foresees trouble and prevents it, is worth two men." But it seemed like the driver didn't feel like listening, because a little while later Uncle Ricardo heard my father say, "No matter where you are going, you don't have to get there first. The thing is, to get there."

And after that he heard my mother say, "Driver, there is more time than life."

And that was all he heard, except for my mother's voice just once more, shouting, "Luisito!" just before my father grabbed me with one hand and threw me out the window.

The bus driver went head-on into another bus. And my mother was right, because time just keeps going on and on and on, but she and my dad and the bus driver and the ticket taker and a lot of other people ran out of life completely.

Uncle Ricardo was okay because he was at the back, and I was okay.

The only part I remember begins with the grip of my father's hand, and how it hurt when he shoved me through the window frame. But I don't like to remember. I like to think about daytime things, my aunts and uncles, and things that are happening now.

But sometimes I still dream about it, being thrown out the window. In the dream I am little again, the same age I was then, and I land down a hillside in a freshly hoed field, just the way I really landed, but it is not daytime, it is almost completely dark, and I get up and go back to the wrecked bus, to find my mom and dad, but it gets darker and darker, and I never can find them.

Uncle Ricardo says one day I won't have the dream anymore. He says that my parents loved me a lot, and that I will always have them in my heart. He says one day my dream self will understand that, too. It will know that my parents are always with me when I remember them. It won't have to go back to the wrecked bus to look for them anymore.

And really I am okay, and Uncle Ricardo is okay, and my grandmother also is okay, because she loves all her children very much, but equally. The only one who has not been okay is my grandfather, because he loved my dad more than anybody. My dad wasn't only his son, he was his best friend.

The first Christmas after the accident we didn't celebrate, because nobody wanted to. But the next Christmas we didn't celebrate either, because Grandpa didn't want to. On the anniversary of the accident, he cut a lot of white roses and put them in front of my parents' wedding picture that hangs in the living room, and we visited their graves at the cemetery, so that was all there was of Christmas that year, too.

And from the beginning my grandmother said we shouldn't mention my mom and dad in front of my grandfather because it might upset him too much. She said we should just wait, and in time he would get better.

But it got to be September of the third year after my father died, and my grandfather still wasn't any better. My aunt Patricia, who had been leaving my cousin Diego with us a lot in Santa Cruz, decided to take Diego to the city. She said it was because she didn't have so many courses and she would have more time to spend with him, but Uncle Ricardo told me it was really because she thought it was too gloomy for Diego around our house.

The only reason I liked being in the house is that I like my grandmother and Celia a lot, my grandmother because she never yells at anybody, and Celia because she treats me like a grown-up. She got me to help her with a lot of projects, especially her Laugh Development Project, in which she said she needed the opinion of a man.

She wanted to develop four new laughs, even though my grandmother said it was a waste of time, and she couldn't see what was wrong with the laugh Celia was born with.

Celia said these are modern times, and a person should have five of everything. She said her original laugh was for when she really felt like laughing, and the other four would be for when she couldn't afford to be serious. She wanted my opinion because she wanted to make sure the four new laughs would be good enough to impress boyfriends.

So when Grandpa wasn't around, she practiced in front of the big cracked mirror on the patio.

"Hah, hah, HAH, HAH, hah," went the first laugh, which is a rapid one where she tosses her long black hair back behind her shoulders. That is her Rio de Janeiro laugh.

"Ho ho ho," she laughs slowly, and rubs her chin thoughtfully with the finger of one hand. That's her Paris laugh.

"Hee hee hee," she giggles, and covers her eyes with her hands. That's her Tahiti laugh.

"Hoo, hoo, hoo, hoo," she laughs, and raises her eyebrows very high. That's her Mexico City laugh.

She got all the ideas for the laughs from TV and from fashion magazines. After she got them all worked out, I told her they were all good, except the Tahiti laugh, which looked like she was just waking up in the morning, so she decided to rename it a waking-up laugh, to throw a stretch into it.

So she did. But just when she had them all perfect, Bright Star got them perfect, too. He sang them all off in a row, and then he said, in my voice, "Laugh Development Project."

"Now I can't bring any boyfriend home!" Celia said. "Either I can't bring one home, or I can't use my laughs."

"Not only that," I said, "Grandpa is going to know about this for sure."

Celia shrugged. "Maybe he'll borrow a laugh," she said. "He doesn't seem to have one of his own. Anyway, what more can he do? We already don't have Christmas anymore."

Sure enough, when Grandpa came home, Bright Star talked. He laughed all four laughs, and then imitated me, saying "Laugh Development Project."

It happened at dinner. My grandfather looked at Bright Star, and he looked at Celia, and he looked at me, but all he said was, "After school tomorrow, I want to take you out to the orchards, Luisito."

So I said okay, and the next afternoon we hiked out to the orchards.

"You are around your Aunt Celia too much," my grandfather said, but not unkindly. "You need the influence of a man."

"I am a man," I said.

"You are?" my grandfather said. "How do you know?"

"Celia said so."

He looked at me and said it took more than Celia's saying so to make somebody a man, and then he started telling me about the trees, and what you had to do to take care of them, and how many different kinds of apples there were, and how you could tell them apart.

But a bad thing happened, because the orchards are right next to the pyramids and the forts of the old kingdom, and I kept thinking about them and wanting to go over there, instead of listening to my grandfather.

"Luisito," he said suddenly, "how many kinds of apples do I have?"

And I couldn't tell him.

"You're not listening! Your father understood and remembered everything when he was your age!" he shouted. "Go on home to your grandmother!"

So I left, and instead of going straight home, I went over to the pyramids and ran up to the top of the biggest and stood there listening to the branches of the pine trees in the wind. It didn't help anything. And then I walked home alone.

When I told my grandma what happened, she said, "Your dad did understand and remember very well when he was your age. But when he was your age, he also played with matches once and set a whole cornfield on fire. It took us, the neighbors and the whole fire department to put it out."

"Tell Grandpa that!" I said. "Remind him about it!"

"I will sometime," my grandmother said, "but not now."

"When?" I asked. "You said Grandpa would get better and we just had to be patient. He used to make jokes, Celia says. He used to take everybody on trips. Now he never does, and he never gets any better."

"You are right," my grandmother said.

"Besides," I said, "Christmas is coming, and I am tired of not having Christmas, and so is Celia."

"You're probably right," my grandmother said. "We should celebrate Christmas."

And she actually used the telephone, which she never uses, to call up Ricardo and talk to him about it.

And that night at dinner, she told my grandfather, "It's time we started to celebrate Christmas again."

"I would rather not," my grandfather said.

"The children say they won't come home for Christmas, unless we celebrate, like the old days. Luis and Celia say they would rather go into the city to be with Ricardo and everybody if we don't celebrate Christmas."

"Um," my grandfather said.

"I might go, too," my grandmother said.

"*You* might go?" my grandfather said.

"Yes, I probably will go," my grandmother said.

"You would *leave* me?" my grandfather said.

"Just for Christmas," my grandmother said.

"It wouldn't be good," my grandfather said. "We've been together thirty-one years. You've never been away. Not one day!"

"Times change," my grandmother said.

"Well," my grandfather said, "we had better celebrate Christmas. But I won't dance."

"You don't have to dance," my grandmother said. "Nobody has to dance. But at least we will have dance music, anyway."

Celia and I made a beautiful golden Christmas tree out of corn husks that we cut to fasten on wires and make the shape of branches. When we were done, the tree went all the way to the ceiling, and we draped it with red chains of tinsel. And my grandmother stood in front of the stove all Christmas Eve day making the tamales for the midnight dinner—corn stuffed with chicken and meat and olives and raisins and hot chili sauce, and wrapped in banana leaves to cook. And everybody arrived from the city about six-thirty at night, just in time for the supper we were going to have to tide us over to the real dinner at midnight.

Uncle Ricardo brought Diego and me about sixty firecrackers to set off at midnight, when all the kids in town go outside to set off firecrackers, so we were feeling good. And my grandfather had dressed up in his best and happiest clothes, new pants, and a cap that makes him look as young as my uncles.

Everybody hugged, and we all sat down to eat, but nobody talked much until we were almost finished, when Aunt Patricia said, "All the same, it's sad anyway."

And my Uncle Pedro, who had been an exchange student in the U.S. for one year of high school, said, "If the roads had shoulders, the way the highways do in the U.S., they never would have died."

And Celia said, "So in the great U.S.A. there are no traffic accidents?"

And before Pedro could answer her, my grandfather got up out of his chair and went out on the patio, and we all stopped talking.

"Luisito," my grandmother said, "go be with your grandfather."

So I went out on the patio and stood by my grandfather, who was looking up at the sky and wouldn't look down.

I just stood there by him, looking up, too.

There was a full moon, shining down on the patio and on the papery violet leaves of the bougainvillea, and my grandfather spoke, in a choked voice.

"See the leaves? There are so many you can't see the branch, and all different.

Ms. Lee made a delighted face. "A house key! Boy! That's a big responsibility for an eight-year-old."

"—for an eight-year-old *wimp,*" whispered Chuck.

Ms. Lee looked at him and pointed to the door. And when he had gone to wait in the anteroom, she drummed her fingers on her chest and looked again at Jesse. "What would you like to say about having a house key?"

"Well, it means you can unlock your own door," said Jesse, in a gentle voice, "—and it means you're growing up."

"Right you are," said Ms. Lee.

One of the older girls dumped a house key out of her loafer onto the rug. "I have one, too," she said. Then, a big boy produced one on a key chain and let it swing from the end of his finger.

"Well, aren't we all growing up!" said Ms. Lee. She paused, looking at the faces of the children. "Anyone else with something?" She glanced at the round clock above the door. "Nobody? Then you are all excused, one minute early, to go home."

The children walked out of the schoolhouse—a few balancing books on their heads on the way down the steps. Jesse was the last to gather his things. Ms. Lee had taken Chuck aside near the door and was holding his arm. Jesse passed slowly by them. "Don't spoil things for the little ones," Ms. Lee was saying. "Leave Hannah alone—she likes to pretend."

"Okay," whined Chuck.

"I mean it, Chuck. There are children of different ages here— "

"I know!"

"Well, act like you know! You happen to be almost three years older than Hannah." She lowered her voice. "And don't you ever call Jesse a wimp. Apparently, he has a bum back—so he's more frail than you are. Count your blessings!"

"Can I go now?"

Ms. Lee released Chuck's arm. "But I'm warning you: ANY more baloney from you and I'm going to MARCH RIGHT OVER to the telephone and call your mother. Understand?"

Chuck fixed his shirt and walked away. He elbowed Jesse on his way down the stairs. "Hannah!" he called. "I have news for you. . . ." He slid down the bannister and jumped to the cement. "The tooth fairy is your mom and dad. Really," he said, in a low voice. "I'm not kidding you."

"My mom and dad?" said Hannah.

"Yes!"

She looked thoughtful. "Then where are their tutus? And where are their wings?"

"Where are whose wings?" said Chuck. He threw up his hands. "Don't you get it?"

Hannah stared at him.

"Your mom and dad take the tooth from under your pillow . . ."

"In some cases!" interrupted Jesse, hurrying over. "In some cases, yes!—as you get older. When you're six or seven—or eight—your mom and dad might be the tooth fairy." He gazed at Hannah. "But when you're four or five—now that's a different matter."

Chuck faked a laugh.

chimney of a can shaped like a cabin. And her whole family walked her to school.

At lunchtime, she sat with Jesse on a bench in the school yard. Jesse opened a bottle of apple juice. He took a swig and passed Hannah the bottle. Hannah had two swallows and passed it back. "I love apple juice," said Hannah. "Thanks."

She handed Jesse a cupcake. "One each," she said. "My dad made them for my birthday."

"Pretty," said Jesse. He undid the pleated paper. "So you're six," he said, licking the frosting off the top.

"Yup."

"Well, you know, Hannah—sometime soon you might have to say good-bye to the tooth fairy."

He drank and passed the bottle.

Hannah drank and passed it back.

"You're growing up!" continued Jesse. "And you lose something by growing up—but you also get something. Since you're older, you get to do things you couldn't—when you were a shrimp. In a way, you lose the tooth fairy like you lose a tooth. There's an empty spot—then something grows to fill it."

"But where does the tooth fairy go?" said Hannah.

"There are places."

"Where?"

Jesse drank exactly half of what was left in the bottle. He paused, looking for words. "Well, let's just say there are places where the sky is torn. Rips—in the blue, where magic leaks in. That's where the tooth fairy comes from. That's where the tooth fairy goes back to."

Hannah looked down at her cupcake. "So, what you mean is—the magic goes away."

Jesse said nothing.

"I hate Chuck," said Hannah.

She finished her cupcake and tossed the wrapper into the trash. "Did I tell you? I got paints for my birthday. And a stuffed bald eagle with a pink felt tongue . . ."

"Good," said Jesse.

"And a plastic calculator with a turtle on it. And a book about Mother Goose." She stood up. "And this dress with dancing apples on it."

"Nice," said Jesse.

Hannah sat back down. "I didn't get a key, though."

"Oh," said Jesse.

They passed the bottle back and forth, each drinking half until there was just a drop left, then half a drop, then none. They sat without speaking. The wind blew some dried leaves in a circle. It caught and flapped in Hannah's hem, turned up her collar, blew back Jesse's bangs. A cloud covered and uncovered the sun.

Ms. Lee rang a bell at the school door and the children returned to the classroom. She stood up behind her large oak desk and said, "This is a special day for somebody in our class."

Hannah's ears turned red.

"Happy birthday, Hannah! Would you like to tell the class how old you are?"

"I'm six," said Hannah.

Chuck leaned close to Hannah. "Well, you can say good-bye to the tooth fairy," he whispered. "At least according to what Jesse says."

Ms. Lee loudly cleared her throat. "After the sharing circle, we'll sing 'Happy Birthday' to Hannah."

Jesse raised his hand. "May I be first to share? It's about Hannah's birthday . . ."

"Oh, gag!" said Chuck.

Ms. Lee cocked an eyebrow and said to him, "That's IT!" Then, she stood up and straightened her skirt and marched out of the room to call Chuck's mother. She poked her head back in. "You may begin," she said to Jesse.

The children arranged themselves on the rug with Jesse in the center. "What are you staring at?" said Chuck. "I couldn't care less if the teacher calls my mother. Just start! You're not the only one with something to share." He grinned—and the gap in the front of his mouth was one tooth wider.

"I have something to show you," said Jesse.

He pulled his sweatshirt over his head and let it drop, inside out, to the floor. He shook loose his curls; his hair was lit from behind—it fell in tangles on his shoulders. Light winked in the red glass rubies on his belt.

Jesse began to undo the snaps on his shirt.

"Ladies and gentlemen," announced Chuck. "For Hannah's birthday, we'll have a strip tease by Jesse The Wimp!"

Jesse ignored him. He slipped off his shirt, so that his arms and chest were bare.

The room grew very quiet. Jesse turned to lay his shirt on the bookshelf.

"Jesse!" cried Hannah. "What's on your back?"

A gust of wind lifted the curtains. The room darkened.

"Yeah, what's on his back?" somebody whispered. "What's going on?"

Jesse glanced over his shoulder at Hannah; her heart fluttered.

"I don't walk the earth," said Jesse softly, turning to face the children. "I fly." And as he spoke, a shaft of sunlight hit Jesse's body; wings, tightly folded on his back, opened like fans behind him—spilling silver dust into the air. They stood erect, majestic and shimmering; silver feathers cut the sunlight into patterns that swirled in circles on the walls.

Jesse looked at Hannah. "You know who I am," he told her. His eyes glittered like black stars.

Some of the children hid their faces in their hands; others were too stunned to speak or move. "You don't have to be afraid," Jesse told them, in a gentle voice.

Like a dark angel, he kneeled in the dust that lay glimmering on the floor.

"You don't have to be afraid," he said again, and touched somebody's hand. "I'm not the only magic thing you've seen." He looked at the faces of the children. "After all, you live in a world where caterpillars turn into butterflies—where pollywogs swim, grow legs . . . hop away."

Chuck began creeping toward the doorway on his hands and knees. Jesse turned and looked at him.

"Hey, Chuck!" he cried. "How much did you get for that last tooth you lost?" Jesse stood up, reached into his pocket, and pulled out a silver dollar.

"Me?" said Chuck, in a very high voice—pointing to himself.

Jesse stared at him.

"Nothing," said Chuck. Then he brightened a little. "Nothing yet, that is. . . ." He crawled over to Jesse and cautiously put out his hand.

Jesse tossed and caught the silver dollar in the air. And tossed and caught it again, glancing at Chuck's hand. "Did you think this was for *you?*" he said, with a laugh.

He turned to Hannah. "Here," he said. "An advance on your bottom two." And he leaned down and pressed it into her palm. "I have to leave you now," Jesse told her, in a whisper.

Hannah stared at the coin without speaking.

Then, Jesse took off the key and put it around Hannah's neck. "Happy birthday, Hannah. Now, you've got the key; you can open any door. You're six, in a world where an egg can turn into a turtle or an eagle. Or a goose! You're growing up, Hannah, on planet Earth—where flowers change into apples, worms into fireflies! And that kind of magic never goes away."

Hannah covered the key with her hand. And when she looked up, Jesse had climbed onto the windowsill and was carefully guiding his wings through the opening. "Jesse?" she whispered, rising. "Jesse—where are you going?"

"I'm so tired!" said Jesse. "I flew all night last night—did you look out your window? Did you see me? And I flew all night the night before. I have to go now—I have to rest." He turned and slid out of the window on his belly, hanging onto the window sash. His wings began to flap—awkwardly at first, and then in a steadier rhythm.

"Wait!" cried Hannah. Wind from Jesse's wings blew back her hair, blew papers from the bookshelf onto the floor.

"Remember me to your baby brother!" called Jesse. And he reached back in through the space to touch Hannah's cheek good-bye.

With his magnificent wings rippling in the sunlight, with his back arched, and his arms stretched upward in a triumphant gesture, Jesse rose into the air.

"Say good-bye to the tooth fairy!" Hannah cried to the other children.

But before they could reach the window, Jesse flew. And Hannah was the only one who saw him travel upward across the sky—swiftly and silently, like a shooting star—and disappear, like a shooting star, into the blue.

Doris Knows Everything

by Whoopi Goldberg
Illustrated by Gary Zamchick

Today I went to the Welfare Office with my mom. My friend Doris said that only really poor people who didn't take baths and ate out of garbage cans were at Welfare.

My friend Doris knows everything.

My friend Doris said that when you get there, there are these big doors and then you have to open them and they're really hard and you have to push until you sweat and then you have to walk down this big long hallway in the dark and they don't even give you a flashlight. And it's really cold in there and they don't even give you a sweater.

My friend Doris said you have to sit on a big tall stool and then they call your name and then you have to go into this room and there's a lady with big glasses and warts and fangs and that's what Doris said.

So I didn't want to go but my mother said I had to and I went. But you know, it looked just like any other building with real regular doors. I said, "Hmmmm."

We went in and there were some chairs and lots of people. I even knew some people. Those people that I knew didn't eat out of garbage cans. Mr. Kellis worked in the school I go to. He smiled and I said hello. I played with my friend Kasha; she was there too. Her mom plays with a symphony, but she got laid off.

And then they called our name and I got scared. And we went in to see a lady named Miss Mason. But she didn't have fangs or warts or glasses or anything. She was kinda pretty.

And I started to think about the things Doris said and I felt pretty silly for listening to her.

So when it was over, me and my mom went to the bathroom 'cause my mom always makes me go to the bathroom right before I leave anywhere because every time we go somewhere I say I have to go to the bathroom. And when we came out of the bathroom, guess who was sitting there with her mom—Doris.

I said, "Hi, Doris." Doris didn't say anything, she just hung her head.

I guess Doris doesn't know everything.

G. ZAMCHICK

Yourself Belongs to You

a rap song by The Fat Boys:
Damon Wimbley, Darren Robinson,
and Mark Morales, with Jimmy Glenn

Take AN-y PATH you WANT to,
  but one THING you OUGHT-a KNOW:
Don't let OTH-ers LEAD you PLACE-es
  YOU don't want to GO!
A DEF thing to re-MEM-ber
  if you DON'T know what to DO:
You GOT a RIGHT to STAND-ing TALL,
  Your-SELF be-LONGS to YOU!

Now . . .

We get ac-CUSED of ACT-in' STU-pid,
  and mak-IN' a LOT-ta NOISE,
But here's SOME-thing REAL SER-ious
  from the THREE FAT BOYS!
Now, one DAY you MIGHT get NERV-ous,
  OR FEEL PRES-sure
FROM SOME-ONE
  who might TRY to TAKE your MEAS-ure!
Some-BOD-y might PUSH you
  TO THE BRINK,
But DON'T BE a-FRAID!
  YO! STOP and THINK
a-BOUT this THING we've LEARNED
  (and WE'LL pass it a-LONG):
TRUST your-SELF! You KNOW the DEAL!
And you'll NEV-er GO WRONG!

You got BOD-y AND SPIR-it!
  WORD! They MAKE YOU u-NIQUE!
Any-ONE tries to de-STROY 'em,
  THEY ARE WEAK!

You got a RIGHT to FEEL GOOD—
  if you're BLUE OR SAD
From SOME-one HIT-tin' ON you—
  THEY'RE the ONE who's BAD!
YO! HURT-in' is con-FUS-in'
  'cause THERE'S so MAN-y WAYS
Other PEOP-le CAN FIND
  to MESS WITH your DAY;
But if they're ILL-in' WITH your HEART
  or BOD-y OR MIND;
If they PUT you in a BIND,
  it's O-ver THE LINE!
So keep UP your CON-fidence
  and DON'T FEEL LOW,
You've GOT a BRAIN like EIN-STEIN,
  JUST LET it SHOW!
You've got a HEART the SIZE of JUP-iter,
  so, CAN'T no-BOD-y HURT ya!
Your HEART's what TELLS you
  YOU ARE RIGHT;
  IT'll NEV-er JERK ya!

Take AN-y PATH you WANT to,
    but one THING you OUGHT-a KNOW:
Don't let OTH-ers LEAD your PLACE-es
    YOU don't want to GO!
A DEF thing to re-MEM-ber
    if you DON'T know what to DO:
You GOT a RIGHT to STAND-ing TALL,
    Your-SELF be-LONGS to YOU!

Just LET the FAT BOYS GIVE you
    a RULE OR TWO,
If some-BOD-y's TOUCH-in'-PULL-in'-
    PICK-in'-HIT-tin' ON YOU—
You don't WANT to be a-LONE?
    GO WITH your CREW!
And IF they STILL are FRONT-in',
    HERE'S WHAT you DO:
Just TELL 'em, "YO! STOP!"
    Then TELL 'em A-GAIN,
You're SICK AND TIRED
    of ALL their MESS-IN'!
And if THAT DON'T WORK,
    get some-ONE you TRUST,

Like your AUNT-ie or your TEACH-er,
    and let THEM MAKE the BUST!

Now we don't SAY when FRIENDS or FAM-i-ly
    MAKE YOU DO
SOME-thing YOU DON'T LIKE
    that they're MIS-TREAT-in' YOU!
They got a RIGHT to TURN you 'ROUND
    if you've GONE A-STRAY,
But if they're TOY-in' WITH your BOD-y,
    DON'T YOU PLAY!
They're like AN-y OTH-er STRANG-er,
    if you're BE-in' A-BUSED;
If the PILL's TOO BIG to SWAL-low,
    JUST RE-FUSE!
So, no MAT-ter WHO IT IS,
    don't TREAT THEM SOFT!
WORD UP, homeboy! GET MAD, flygirl!
    TELL 'em, "STEP OFF!"
'Cause WHEN the HEAT is IN your HOUSE,
    THAT'S the HOT-test YET,
So, go ELSE-where to GET re-LIEF;
But GET IT! BET!
What's RIGHT is RIGHT in BLACK and WHITE,
    NOTH-in' ELSE will DO.
You GOT a RIGHT to STAND-ing TALL,
    Your-SELF be-LONGS to YOU!

Lily Tomlin's Edith Ann in "And That's the Truth"

written and illustrated by Jane Wagner

"God has a TV set and
watches us on it.
Whenever I feel God
watching me,
I sing and dance and do
a commercial for myself."

"Sometimes when I feel nobody cares…
I go down to Sears and tell them
I'm lost and they call my name out
over the loudspeaker over and over.

We all need to feel like we matter.

I matter to Sears even though most of my clothes
come from J.C. Penney."

On My Pond

Words and Music by Kermit the Frog
with Sarah Durkee and Christopher Cerf
Illustrations by Tom Cooke

♪ music on page 236

There's a place where I can sit,
   just me, myself and I . . .
On my pond,
On my pond

Where the water's fresh and clean
   and peaceful as a sigh . . .
On my pond,
On my pond

Look at the grass all around me,
It's green as the smile on my face,
Look at the trees, they astound me!
Wow, what a byoo-tiful plaaace!

There's a spot where no one lives
    but quiet little fish . . .
On my pond,
On my pond.

Nature lets me come and visit
    any time I wish . . .
On my pond,
On my pond.

Look at us ALL, . . .
     we're enjoying
A breath of sweet country air . . .
Hey, this is getting ANNOYING!
PLEASE KEEP IT DOWN OVER THEEEERE . . . !

WAIT A MINUTE, WHO SAID YOU COULD
     DUMP YOUR GARBAGE HERE? . . .
On my pond,
On my pond.

CLEANIN' IT ALL UP AGAIN
     COULD TAKE US YEARS AND YEARS . . .
On my pond,
On my pond.

Keepin' it clean to BEGIN WITH!
Yes, that's the smart thing to do!
Don't let 'em cover our fins with
Any more black slimy gooooo . . . !

Save a place where I can sit,
  just me, myself and I. . . .
On my pond,
On my pond.

Keep the water fresh and clean
  and peaceful as a sigh . . .
On my pond,
On my pond!

All Us Come Cross the Water

by Lucille Clifton
Illustrated by John Steptoe

I got this teacher name Miss Wills. This day she come asking everybody to tell where they people come from. Everybody from over in the same place suppose to stand up by theirselves. When it come to me I don't say nothing so she get all mad, cause that make all the other brothers not say nothing too.

"Won't you please cooperate with us, Jim?" she say. I didn't say nothing cause my name is Ujamaa for one thing. So when the bell ring she ask me to stay a little after, so we can talk.

"We must not be ashamed of ourselves, Jim," she says. "You are from a great heritage and you must be proud of that heritage. Now you know you are from Africa, don't you?" she says.

I say, "Yes, mam," and walk on out the place.

First thing, my name is Ujamaa and also Africa is a continent not a country and she says she want everybody to tell what country. Anyhow, I left. The other brothers waiting for me by the light.

Malik say, "That woman is crazy. She get on my nerves."

Bo say, "How come we didn't stan up, Ujamaa? We from Africa!" I just go on home. Bo don't know nothing.

I got a sister name Rose. She studying to be a practical nurse. When she get home I ask her, "Rose where we from?" She come talking about, "Mama was from Rome, Georgia, and Daddy from Birmingham."

"Before that," I say.

"Mama's Daddy from Georgia too."

"I mean before that too, way back before that." She come laughing talking about, "They wasn't no way back before that. Before that we was a slave."

Rose make me sick.

My Daddy's name Nat. He work for the city. When he get home I ask him, "Daddy where we from?"

He say, "What you talking about, boy?"

I say, "I wanna know where did we come from."

Everyone looked relaxed and nobody was particularly peeved. That was because they were used to it. Most of the many automobile accidents in the kingdom with no rules and no laws resulted in people hanging by one leg, upside down, in trees.

As Benjamin swayed in the breeze, he could see a baseball field in the distance. A game was in progress, a game with no rules, of course. The players were doing whatever they felt like doing. Some were swinging bats. Some were throwing balls. Some were catching balls.

Some were running back and forth on the bases bumping into each other. Some were helping the injured off the field.

There was no score for some, and for others it was 12 to 6 or 765 to 125 and so on.

For some a hit was a hit, for others a hit was an out, and for a few there was no such thing as a hit or an out.

Some just sort of sat there in the middle of the base paths, digging in the dirt with pails and shovels.

"THERE'S GOT TO BE A BETTER WAY!" Benjamin was screaming over and over as they carried him down from the tree.

"It's okay, Benjamin, dear. You're down now," his mother said. "We're all okay now. We're out of our trees. See. We're out of our trees!"

Benjamin looked around and saw that everyone was, indeed, out of their trees. And it was at that very moment that he resolved to himself he would figure out a better way.

"I'm going to my room and I'm not coming out until I'm finished!" Benjamin said.

"Finished with what?" his sister asked.

"I don't know yet," he said, slamming the door behind him.

News spread all over the kingdom that a boy named Benjamin had gone to his room and wouldn't come out until he was finished. The entire kingdom gathered around Benjamin's house waiting for him to come out of his room with whatever it was that he was finishing.

Then, after two and a half hours, Benjamin emerged.

"Finished!" he said.

"Finished *what*?" the kingdom asked.

"Three laws and a bunch of rules," he said proudly.

"Huh?" said the kingdom, not having the faintest idea what he was talking about.

"This is the bunch of rules," Benjamin explained, holding up a booklet. "From now on, we'll play baseball by the rules in this book, like nine people on each side, nine innings, four balls, three strikes, no pails and shovels, stuff like that. If you don't play by these rules, you can't play."

"Interesting!" some of the people in the kingdom said.

"Sounds pretty good," others said.

"No pails and shovels? Phooey!" said Benjamin's mother and father and some others.

"Get to the three laws!" his sister demanded impatiently.

"Yeah!" said the kingdom.

"Okay," Benjamin said, and he took out a very impressive piece of notebook paper and began to read:

"Everyone will stop on red and go on green. That's the first law.

"Nobody can take another person's chocolate ice cream cone. That's the second law.

"Every day at noon, the entire kingdom has to come over to my house, play cowboy, dig in my sandbox with pails and shovels, and sing and dance to a great song I wrote called 'Hail Benjamin, He's a Heck of a Guy!' That's the third law. If you don't obey the laws, you get punished."

"Interesting," some of the people in the kingdom said.

"Sounds pretty good!" others said.

"The law with the pails and shovels is my favorite," said Benjamin's mother and father.

"Hail *who*?" said a guy in the back to no one in particular.

Then Benjamin said that he was going back to his room and he would not come out until the kingdom tried the three laws and the bunch of rules.

So they did. And they found that they no longer spent as much time hanging by one leg, upside down, in trees. They were able to finish their chocolate ice cream cones, and baseball was a lot more fun. But every day at noon, not everyone was coming over to Benjamin's house and playing cowboy, digging, and singing and dancing like they were supposed to.

"I can't. I have an earache," one guy said.

"I'm allergic," said another guy.

"My pail and shovel are at the cleaners," Ben's sister said.

"Oh yeah?" said Benjamin. "Prove it. Show me doctors' notes and a pail-and-shovel cleaning ticket."

The two guys had notes, but Benjamin's sister didn't have a pail-and-shovel cleaning ticket. She said she'd lost it. Then she said, "Okay, look. I don't like the third law. I don't see why, every day at noon, everyone has to come all the way over to our house and play cowboy, dig, and sing and dance to 'Hail Benjamin, He's a Heck of a Guy!' "

"We have to because it's the law," the kingdom tried to explain.

"But it's a *silly* law. It serves no useful purpose," Benjamin's sister replied.

"True," Benjamin said. "But I like it a lot. It's a *fun* law!"

His parents agreed.

"I don't think it's fun!" Benjamin's sister said. "I don't like it one bit."

"You don't?" Benjamin asked.

"No, I don't!" said his sister.

To Benjamin's genuine surprise, more than a few of the people in the kingdom appeared to agree with her.

"Okay, no problem," Benjamin said with a shrug. "From now on, the law is: Every day at noon, *no one's* allowed to come over to our house and do *anything*."

"Brilliant! Hooray for Benjamin!" cheered everyone in the kingdom. Everyone except Benjamin's sister, that is.

"Wait a minute! That's no good either!" she shouted, taking a deep breath. "We don't need a law to force people to come over to our house and play cowboy and dig and sing and stuff like that, but we also shouldn't have one to *stop* them from doing it if they feel like it."

"We shouldn't?" the kingdom asked.

"No," she said. "As long as no harm comes to anyone, why should there be a law against it?"

"You know, she has a point," said her mother and father.

"A very *good* point!" a lot of other people in the kingdom joined in.

So the kingdom kept the first and second laws and the bunch of rules, but got rid of the third law altogether. They also decided that from then on, *all* the people would be involved in making laws and rules because, after all, stuff like that was just too important to be left to some guy in a cowboy hat.

Benjamin eventually became a very successful singing cowboy. His sister became senior partner of the kingdom's first law firm. His parents became umpires. And the kingdom that now had *some* laws and *some* rules lived lawfully ever after. It still had no king . . . but it's too late to get into that now.

THE END

The Turn of the Tide

*Words and Music by Carly Simon
and Jacob Brackman
Illustrated by John Steptoe*

♪ music on page 238

How can we know
   the fate of the earth?
Must everything go
   from bad to worse?
How can we be
   just along for the ride?
We'd rather believe
   that WE decide!
That we can stand here
And say loud and clear:
   Here comes the turn of the tide.

184

Here comes the turn,
Here comes the turn,
Here comes the turn of the tide.

We cannot go on
  sounding alarms
And rattling swords
  and building bombs
And fouling the air
  and the streams underground.
We've got to begin
  to turn it around!
It's our right to be heard,
Our right to decide—
Here comes the turn of the tide.

Here comes the turn,
Here comes the turn,
Here comes the turn of the tide.

We Need a Bigger Turkey

by Christopher Cerf and Norman Stiles
Illustrated by Chris Demarest

One day my dad took Mom and Sid
And Sue and me aside,
And he said, "Let's have a party!
Hey! Let's show our family pride!
We've got such a loving family!
We've got lots to celebrate!
So let's eat the biggest turkey
That five people ever ate!"

Then Dad telephoned our butcher
(Who's a woman named Marie),
And he told her 'bout the turkey
And how big it had to be.

"Sounds great!" said Mom, when Dad hung up,
"But I don't think it's fair
To have a family feast
If Gramps and Grandma aren't there."
"Good point!" said Sue, "and how 'bout
Aunt Elaine and Uncle Gus?
Last time *they* served a turkey
They invited all of *us.*"

"You're right, of course," my father said,
"And when you add each cousin,
The number in our party
Will have reached an even dozen."

So Dad called back the butcher,
And he passed along the word;
"Gonna need a bigger turkey!
Gonna need a larger bird!
'Cause the guest list for our dinner
Has had seven added to it.
Please, Marie, ya gotta help us!"
And the butcher said, "I'll do it!"

Just then, my little brother Sid
Began to scream and pout.
He said, "Dad, I love our babysitter!
Please don't leave her out!"
"And we've *got* to ask the neighbors,"
Mother added lovingly.
"Sure, I know we're not *related,*
But they're family to me!"

So Dad called up the butcher,
And he said, "Remember me?
Well, we need a bigger turkey,
We'll be feeding fifty-three!"

And the butcher said, "No problem!
Hey, don't sweat it, have no fear!
You need a bird for fifty-three?
I've got that bird right here!"

Then Sue brought up the club she runs
That works for conservation,
And Dad his bowling league,
And Mom her Children's Aid Foundation.
And we thought of tons of other folks
We all hold close and dear.
Said Dad, "No doubt about it,
All those people should be here!"

So he called the butcher up and sighed,
"I hate to be a bother,
But it seems our party's grown again.
I'm sorry!" said my father.

"We're gonna host a thousand people,
Give or take a few.
We need a bigger turkey,
And it all depends on you!"

And the butcher said, "I've *just* the bird
To feed the guests you've got.
Your turkey got here yesterday.
It's in the parking lot!"

Well, everyone seemed pleased,
But then I said, "For what it's worth,
The *world* is one big family
'Cause we all share *just one earth*."

"Good point!" said Mom and Dad,
"Our party won't be a success
Unless we invite *everyone*,
And everyone says yes."

So Dad called back the butcher,
And she said, "Now let me guess.
You need a bigger turkey?"
And my father answered, "Yes.

"A bird to feed five billion mouths
Or more before we're through."
"No bird's that big," the butcher sighed,
"I'm sorry. No can do!"

We all burst into tears
When we heard about the call,
And how the largest turkey
In the world was still too small.

But suddenly my mom cried, "Wait!
We won't throw in the towel!
If we can't *buy* the bird we need,
We'll make our *own* big fowl!"

Well, it's taken years of carving,
And of ordering from delis,
But at last we've got a gobbler
That'll fill five billion bellies.
So, world, you're all invited,
Come by air, land, sea, or river,
And taste the biggest turkey
Ever sculpted from chopped liver!

We and They

by Lucille Clifton
Illustrated by Jerry Pinkney

Boris and Yuki and Sarah and Sue
and Karl and Latanya, Maria too
dreamed of the world
and it was spinning
and all the people
just talked about winning.
The wind was burning.
The water was churning.
The trees were bending.
Something was ending
and all the talk was "we" and "they."
The children all hugged themselves
waiting for the day
when the night of the long bad dream
is done
and all the family of humans
are one
and being and winning are not the same
and "we" and "they" is just a game
and the wind is a friend that
doesn't fuss
and every They is
actually Us.

Thank Someone

Words by Sarah Durkee, Music by Paul Jacobs
Illustrated by James McMullan

♪ see page 239 for the music

Mom put down the paper
just to help me find my shoe.
Kim likes chocolate doughnuts,
so her cousin gave her two.
Grampa played with Julio,
took him to the park.
If you forgot to thank someone,
say thank you in the dark.

Thank the moon,
thank the sun,
most of all
Thank someone.
Thank the stars
high above,
one for
everyone you love.

Gretchen taught a funny song
to Jack and Eleanor.
Ed brought Andy comics
when he had to stay indoors.
Mrs. Rose helped Dana
when she waded out too deep.
If you forgot to thank someone,
say thank you in your sleep.

Thank the moon,
thank the sun,
most of all
Thank someone.
Thank the stars
high above,
one for
everyone you love.

Friends are like a family,
and families are like friends.
All the world's your family;
the chain will never end.
When the night is lonely
and we're feelin' miles apart,
if you forgot to thank someone
say thank you in your heart.

Thank the moon,
thank the sun,
most of all
Thank someone.
Thank the stars
high above,
one for
everyone you love.

The Biggest Problem
(Is in Other People's Minds)

Words and Music by Don Haynie
Illustrated by Simms Taback

♪ music on page 235

My brother Bobby never listens when I talk;
Pays close attention though, and watches like a hawk.
Took some time for my hands to learn the signs,
But now the two of us, we get along just fine.

Bobby's biggest problem is in other people's minds;
We do things we like to do and have a great time.
Some kids stay away, but if they knew him they would find
Bobby's biggest problem really is in other people's minds.

I've known Rosa for a year or so by now;
We've been all around, I sometimes wonder how.
The doors and the stairs give us trouble with her chair;
It may take longer, but we go everywhere.

Rosa's biggest problem is in other people's minds;
We go where we want to go and have a great time.
Since this city's builders didn't think when they designed,
Rosa's biggest problem really is in other people's minds.

Rosa

Angie reads to me the poetry she loves;
Hands brush the pages with the gentleness of doves.
Sings me a song from the piano clear and strong,
She's never seen me, yet she's known me all along.

Angie's biggest problem is in other people's minds;
We go hiking, we go swimming, in the summer sunshine.
Anyone can see I'm lucky she's a friend of mine,
And that Angie's biggest problem is in other people's minds.

Sometimes the biggest problem is in other people's minds;
Be exactly who you are, and you'll do just fine.
Things may look impossible, but try and you will find
That the biggest problem really is in other people's, other people's—
Someday we will change those people's minds!

What Are Little Boys Made Of?

by Elaine Laron
drawing by Max Burgle, age 7

What are little boys made of, made of?
What are little boys made of?
Love and care
And skin and hair
That's what little boys are made of.

What are little girls made of, made of?
What are little girls made of?
Care and love
And (SEE ABOVE)
That's what little girls are made of.

William's Doll

Music by Mary Rodgers **Lyric by Sheldon Harnick**
Adapted from the book, William's Doll *by Charlotte Zolotow*

When my friend Wil-liam was five years old He wan-ted a doll__ to hug and hold. "A

doll," said Wil-liam, "is what I need to wash and clean and dress and feed; A doll to

give a bot-tle to___ And put to bed when day_ is through;_ And a-ny time my doll_ gets

Am9   Fmaj7   Dm7   A7sus4 Dm7   G9sus4

ill,   I'll   take good care— of it,"— said my friend

A♭maj7   A♭6   E7/G♯   A♭6   A♭7   A♭   A♭7-5   A♭

Bill.   "A   doll!— a doll!— Wil- liam wants a   doll!"

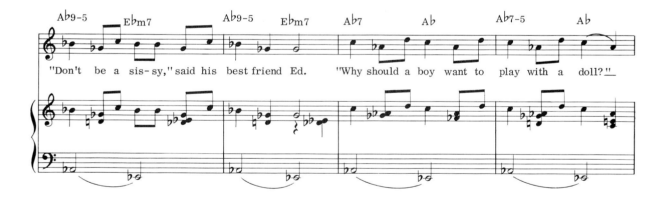

A♭9-5   E♭m7   A♭9-5   E♭m7   A♭7   A♭   A♭7-5   A♭

"Don't   be a sis-sy," said his best friend Ed.   "Why should a boy want to   play with a   doll?"—

G♭7   G♭+/D♭   G♭7-5   G♭7   F

"Dolls are for girls," said his cou- sin Fred.   "Don't be a jerk," said his   ol- der broth-er,—

"I know what to do," said his fa-ther to his moth-er. So his

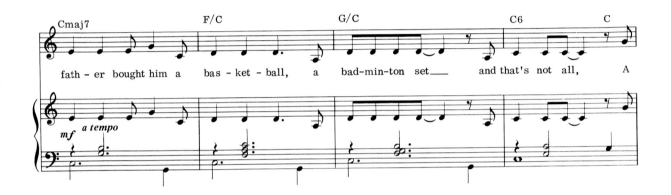

fath-er bought him a bas-ket-ball, a bad-min-ton set___ and that's not all, A

bag of mar-bles, a base-ball glove and all the things___ a boy would love. And Bill was

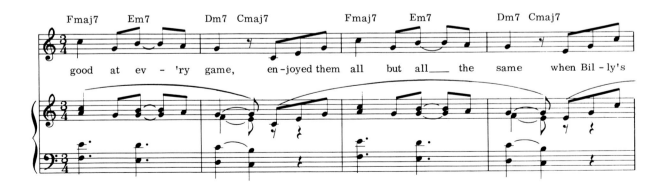

good at ev-'ry game, en-joyed them all but all___ the same when Bil-ly's

198

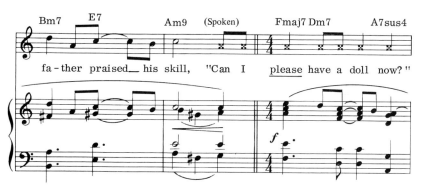

fa-ther praised__ his skill, "Can I please have a doll now?"

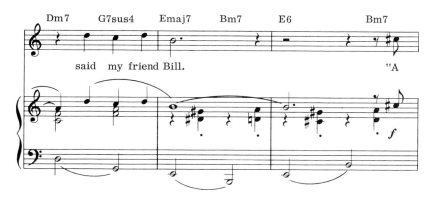

said my friend Bill. "A

doll!__ A doll!__ Wil-liam wants a doll!__ A doll!__ A doll!__ Wil-liam wants a doll!" Then

Wil-liam's grand-ma ar-rived one day and want-ed to know__ what he liked to play. And

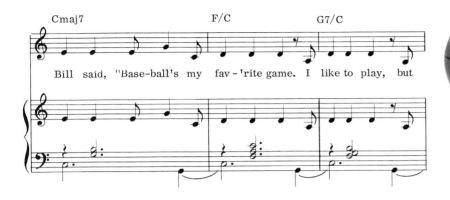

Bill said, "Base-ball's my fav-'rite game. I like to play, but

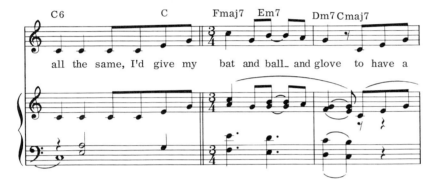

all the same, I'd give my bat and ball and glove to have a

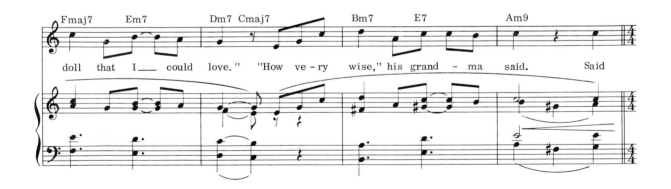

doll that I could love." "How ve-ry wise," his grand-ma said. Said

Bill, "But ev-'ry one_____ says this in-stead!: 'A

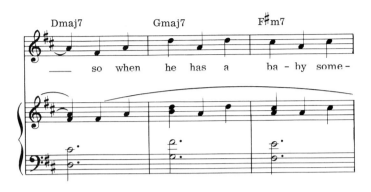

Dmaj7   Gmaj7   F#m7

so when he has a ba - by some-

Waltz feeling

B7sus4   B7   Em

day_____ he'll know how to

Em(maj7)   Em7

dress it, put dia-pers on dou-ble, and gen-tly ca-ress it to

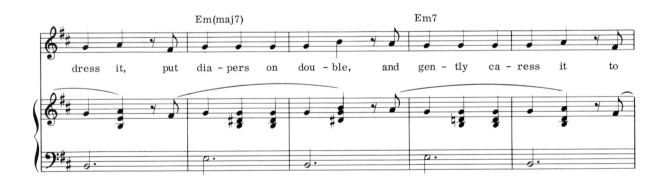

A9   Bm   Bm(maj7)

bring up a bub-ble, and care for his ba-by as ev-'ry good

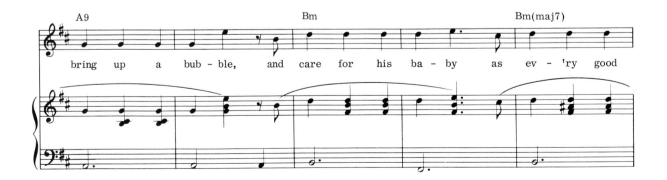

fa - ther should learn   to   do.____

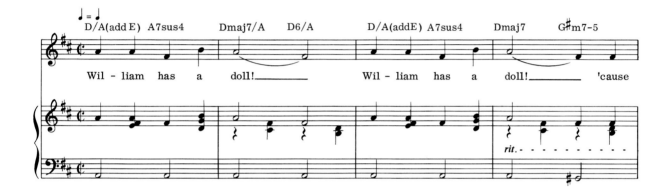

Wil - liam has a doll!____   Wil - liam has a doll!____   'cause

rit. - - - - - - - - -

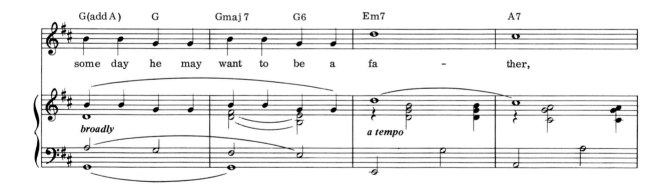

some day he may want to be a fa - ther,

broadly

a tempo

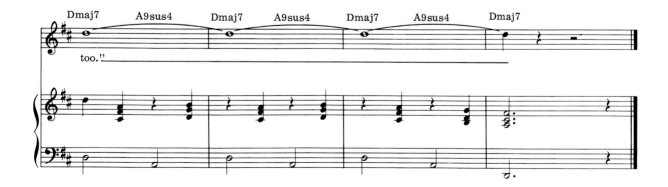

too."____

Sisters and Brothers

Helping

by Shel Silverstein

Freely

A-ga-tha Fry she made a pie, and Chris-toph-er John helped bake it.__

Chris-toph-er John he mowed the lawn, and A-ga-tha Fry helped rake it.__

Za-cha-ry Zugg took out the rug, and Jen-ni-fer Joy helped shake it. And

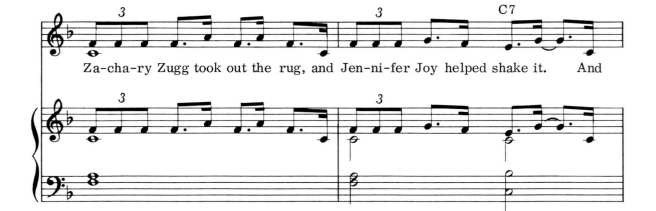

Jen-ni-fer Joy she made a toy, and Za-cha-ry Zugg helped break it.__ And

some kind of help is the kind of help that help-ing's all a-bout. And

some kind of help is the kind of__ help we all can do with-out.

Free To Be . . . A Family

Music by Paul Jacobs, Words by Sarah Durkee

Free To Be . . . You And Me

Music by Stephen Lawrence, Lyric by Bruce Hart

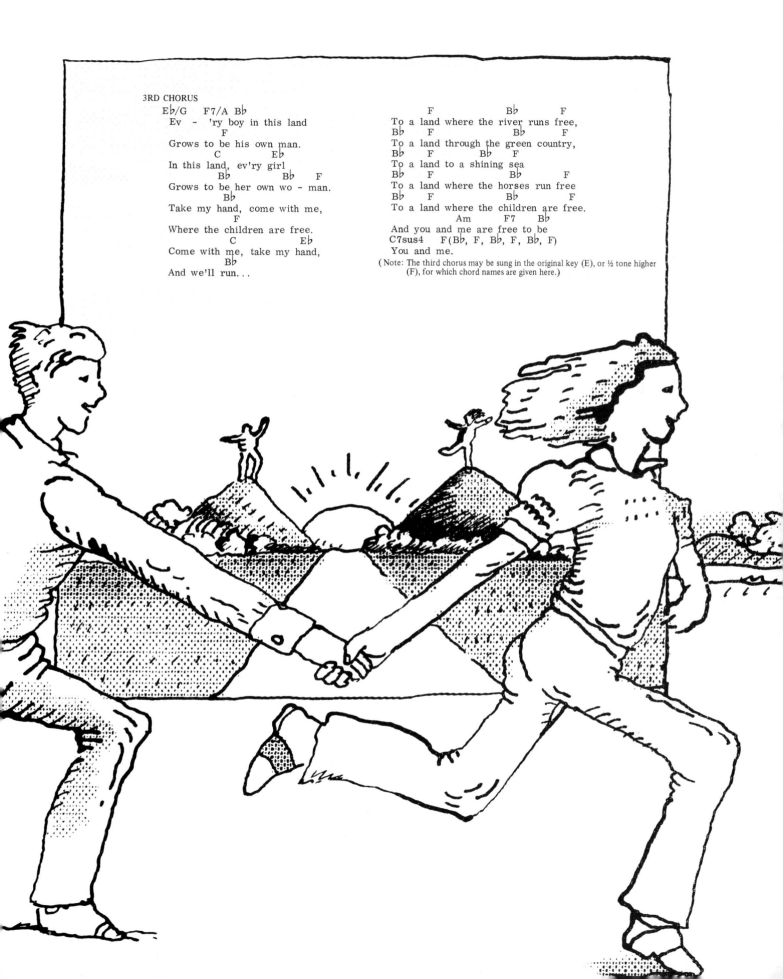

3RD CHORUS

Eb/G   F7/A Bb
Ev - 'ry boy in this land
       F
Grows to be his own man.
       C   Eb
In this land, ev'ry girl
       Bb   Bb   F
Grows to be her own wo - man.
         Bb
Take my hand, come with me,
       F
Where the children are free.
       C   Eb
Come with me, take my hand,
       Bb
And we'll run...

     F   Bb   F
To a land where the river runs free,
Bb   F   Bb   F
To a land through the green country,
Bb   F   Bb   F
To a land to a shining sea
Bb   F   Bb   F
To a land where the horses run free
Bb   F   Bb   F
To a land where the children are free.
         Am   F7   Bb
And you and me are free to be
C7sus4   F(Bb, F, Bb, F, Bb, F)
You and me.

(Note: The third chorus may be sung in the original key (E), or ½ tone higher
(F), for which chord names are given here.)

Parents Are People

by Carol Hall

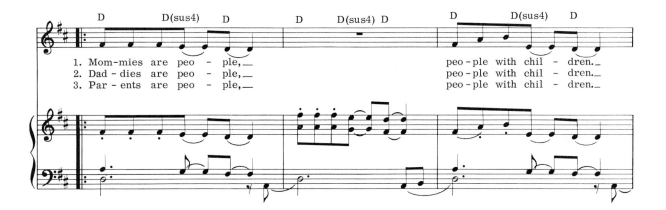

1. Mom-mies are peo - ple,— peo - ple with chil - dren.—
2. Dad - dies are peo - ple,— peo - ple with chil - dren.—
3. Par - ents are peo - ple,— peo - ple with chil - dren.—

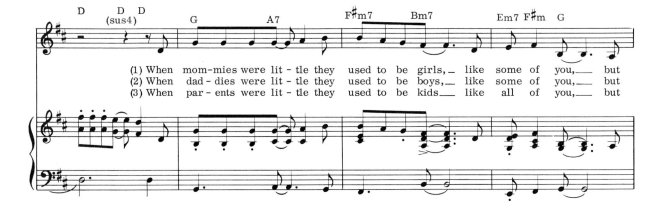

(1) When mom-mies were lit - tle they used to be girls,— like some of you,— but
(2) When dad - dies were lit - tle they used to be boys,— like some of you,— but
(3) When par - ents were lit - tle they used to be kids— like all of you,— but

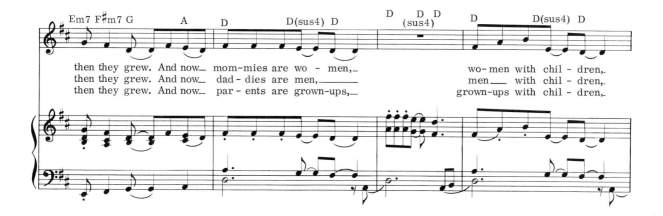

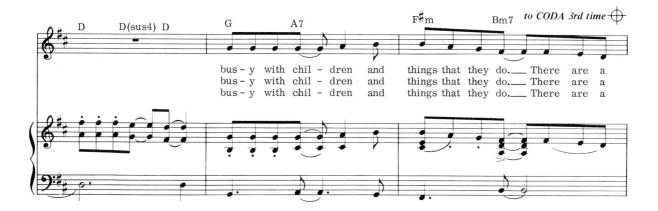

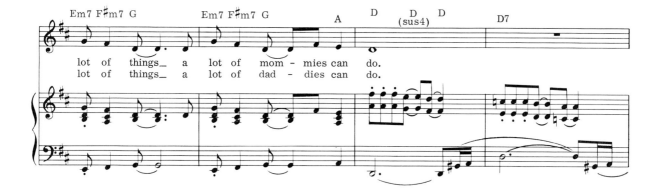

Some mom-mies are ranch-ers or po-et-ry mak - ers__ or
Some dad-dies are writ-ers or gro-cer-y sell - ers__ or

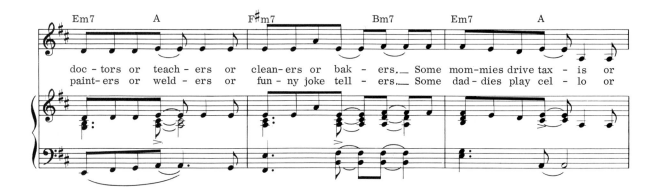

doc - tors or teach-ers or clean-ers or bak - ers.__ Some mom-mies drive tax - is or
paint-ers or weld-ers or fun - ny joke tell - ers.__ Some dad-dies play cel - lo or

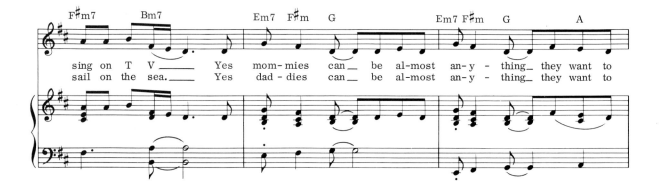

sing on T V ____ Yes mom-mies can__ be al-most an-y - thing__ they want to
sail on the sea.____ Yes dad-dies can__ be al-most an-y - thing__ they want to

218

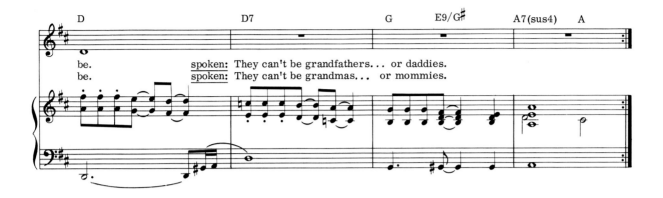

be.   spoken: They can't be grandfathers... or daddies.
be.   spoken: They can't be grandmas... or mommies.

CODA

lot of things_ a lot of mom - mies and a lot of dad - dies and a lot of par - ents can_

do._

219

When We Grow Up

Music by Stephen Lawrence, Lyric by Shelley Miller

Moderately, not too slowly

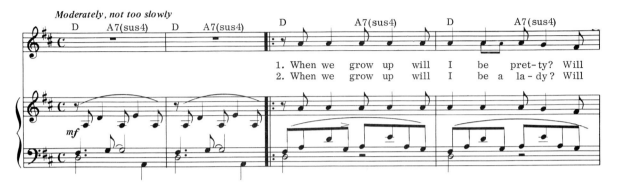

1. When we grow up will I be pret-ty? Will
2. When we grow up will I be a la - dy? Will

you be big and strong?___ Will I wear dress-es that
you be on the moon?___ Well, it might be all right to

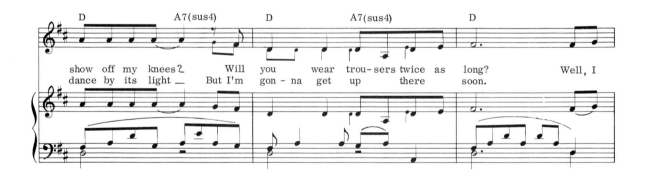

show off my knees? Will you wear trou-sers twice as long? Well, I
dance by its light ___ But I'm gon-na get up there soon.

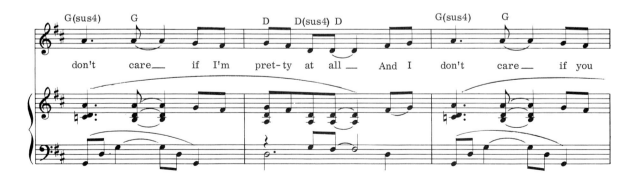

don't care___ if I'm pret-ty at all ___ And I don't care___ if you

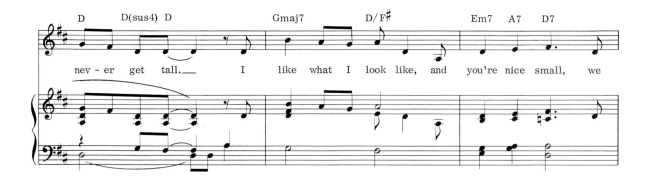

nev - er get tall.___ I like what I look like, and you're nice small, we

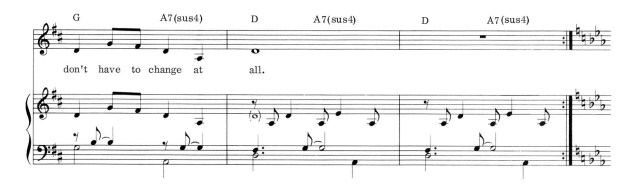

don't have to change at all.

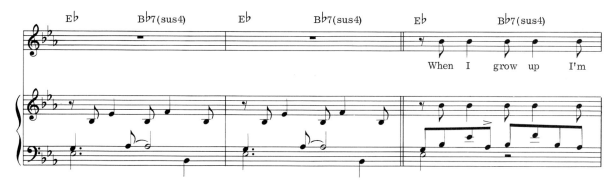

When I grow up I'm

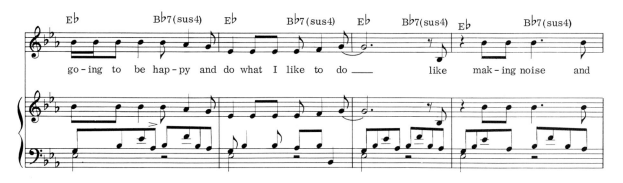

go - ing to be hap - py and do what I like to do ___ like mak - ing noise and

mak-ing fac - es and mak-ing friends like you. And when we grow up___ do you

think___we'll see___ that I'm still like you___ and you're still___ like me?___

freely

I might be pret - ty, you might grow tall. But we don't have to change at

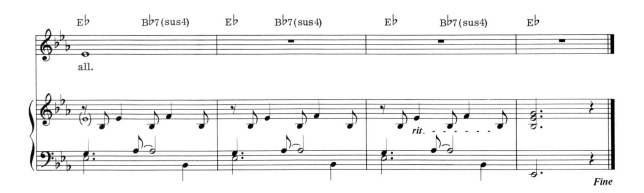

all.

Fine

It's All Right to Cry

by Carol Hall

It's all right to cry,
Cry - ing gets the sad out of you. It's all right to
Rain-drops from your eyes, Wash-ing all the mad out of you. Rain-drops from your

cry, It might make you feel bet-ter.
eyes, It might make you feel bet-ter. It's all right to

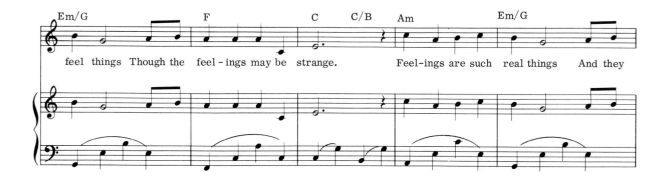

feel things Though the feel-ings may be strange. Feel-ings are such real things And they

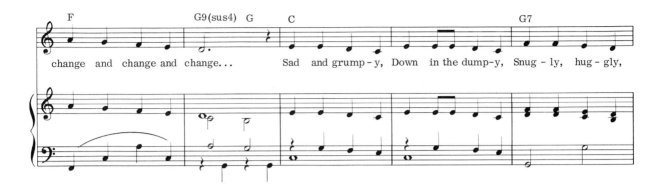

change and change and change... Sad and grump-y, Down in the dump-y, Snug-ly, hug-gly,

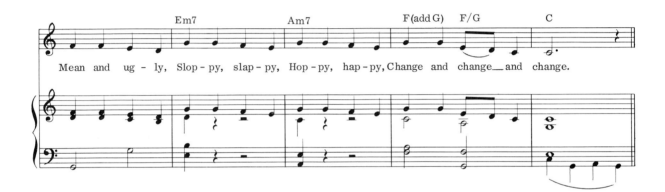

Mean and ug-ly, Slop-py, slap-py, Hop-py, hap-py, Change and change__ and change.

It's all right to know, Feel-ings come and feel-ings go, And it's all right to

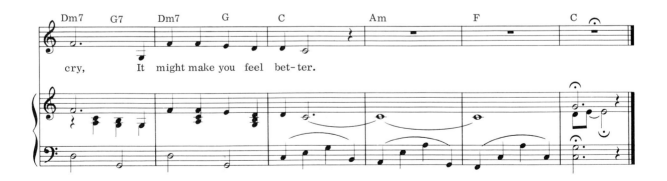

cry, It might make you feel bet-ter.

It's Not My Fault

Words and Music by Sarah Durkee and Christopher Cerf

Glad to Have a Friend Like You

by Carol Hall

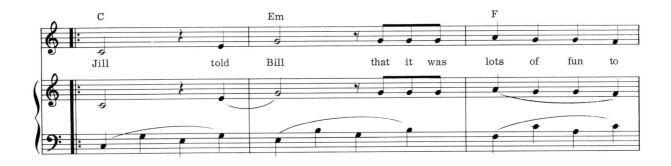

Jill told Bill that it was lots of fun to

cook. Bill told Jill that she could bait a real fish-

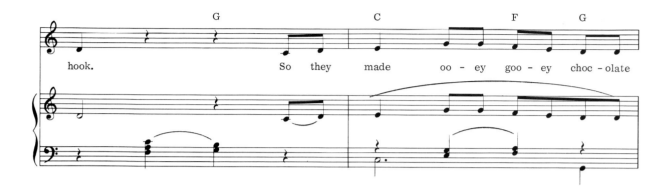

hook.   So   they   made   oo - ey   goo - ey   choc - olate

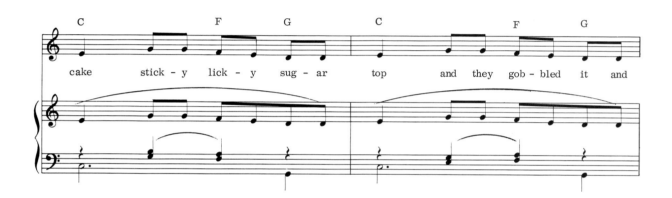

cake   stick - y   lick - y   sug - ar   top   and   they   gob - bled   it   and

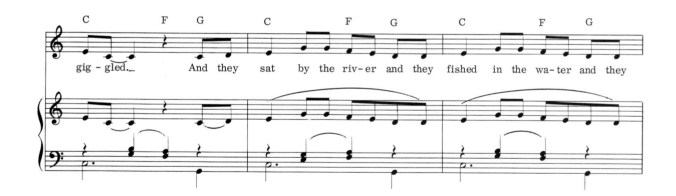

gig - gled.___   And   they   sat   by   the   riv - er   and   they   fished   in   the   wa - ter   and   they

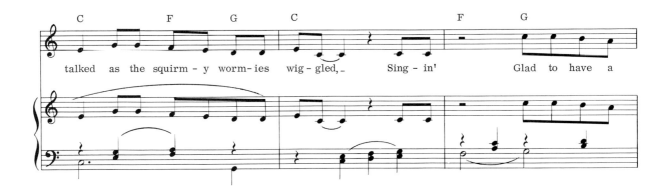

talked as the squirm - y worm - ies wig - gled, — Sing - in' Glad to have a

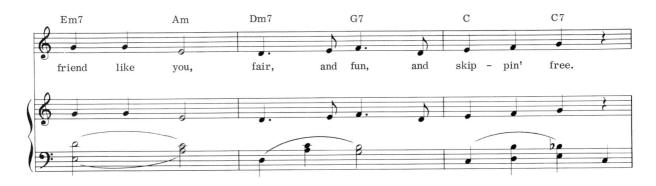

friend like you, fair, and fun, and skip - pin' free.

F   G   Em7   Am   Dm   G7

Glad to have a friend like you, and glad to just be

1, 2   3
C   F   G   C   F   G   Dm7   G7   Dm7   G

me.   Glad to just be, glad to just be

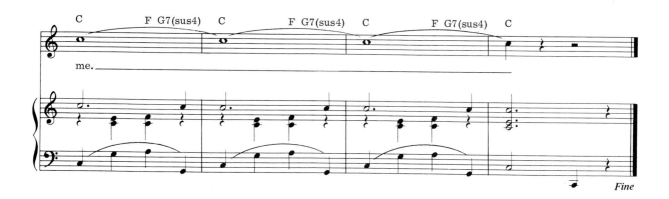

C   F   G7(sus4)   C   F   G7(sus4)   C   F   G7(sus4)   C

me. _____

Fine

Friendly Neighborhood

Words and Music by Lynn Ahrens and Stephen Flaherty

My fam- ily be- gan with Mom and Dad and Sam and me. Then Mom and Dad di- vorced, and, boy, I cried! 'Cause sud- den- ly, in- stead of four, my fam- ily felt like three, and it took a lit- tle while 'til Sam and me could see that what we'd real- ly done was mul- ti- plied. Mom got

1. mar- ried to a fel- la and I got to catch the flow- ers at the wed- ding. Well, we like him, and we call him Ted the Bear. Ted has three kids from when he used to be the hus- band of A- li- cia, and they vis- it us on week- ends, and he takes us ev- 'ry- where. (spoken:) And let me tell you, We really have to squish into that car. It's a tight squeeze. And Dad met

2. Mar- sha. She's a law- yer. And I think they're get- ting mar- ried. Her two kids are both a- dopt- ed, and they come from Vi- et- nam. So that makes Mom and Ted the Bear, and Dad and Mar- sha and A- li- cia, Three new broth- ers, two new sis- ters, and my creep- y broth- er Sam. (spoken:) I think Sam is still a little shy around girls. Well, he's just little.

3. ev- en count- ing cous- ins, 'cause by now there must be doz- ens. Some are young- er, some are old- er, I mean, cous- sins by the ton! And as for hav- ing aunts and un- cles, well, the list would take me hours, but at hol- i- days and birth- days, gee, the crowd is real- ly fun! (spoken:) Except, of course, you have to get kissed and hugged a whole lot more. Ugh!

2. I'm older! And there's Gram, good old Gram, and there's Grand- pa Hen- ry, al- so Grand- ma Ann- ie, plus an ex- tra

230

Jimmy Says
Words and Music by David Buskin and Abra Bigham

In My Room

Words and Music by Bobby Gosh

I'm Never Afraid

Words and Music by Sarah Durkee and Christopher Cerf

♩=125 Uptempo Country Rock

VERSE

1. Some-times I'm a-fraid of what would hap-pen to me if
2. An-nie's scared of heights and Dan's a-fraid of snakes and I'm
3. moth-er's got a friend who likes to hug me a lot, yeah, he's

some-one came and took me a-way. And some-times I'm a-fraid of stuff that's
scared to pass the bul-ly next door. And some-times I'm a-fraid they'll make a
nice to me be-yond a doubt. But if some-bod-y hugs me and it

on T V, or wor-ried if my mom's o-kay. And
stu-pid mis-take and some-one'll start a nu-cle-ar war! But
bugs me a lot, I say "Mom, they've got-ta CUT THAT OUT!" You

some-times I'm so scared a-bout the mon-sters in my clos-et I
once this kid was brag-gin' 'bout a brand new bike he was
might be scared the truth is gon-na make 'em mad, and you're

hard-ly ev-en dare to blink. But one thing I can tell you you should
plan-nin' to go out and steal. I said, "It's dumb to do that!" and I
pet-ri-fied to have a fight, But come right out and say it and you

nev-er be a-fraid of is say-in' what you real-ly think!
was-n't a-fraid 'cause I told him how I real-ly feel! } Oh, no, I'm
won't be a-fraid, if you're say-in' what you know is right!

CHORUS

nev-er a-fraid, I'm nev-er a-fraid to say what's on my mind! No, I'm

nev-er a-fraid, I'm nev-er a-fraid to say what's on my mind! There's

all kinds of brave and all kinds of cour-age-ous, But me I'm the brav-est kind, 'cause I'm

Fine

1.

nev-er a-fraid to say what's on my mind! Well,

233

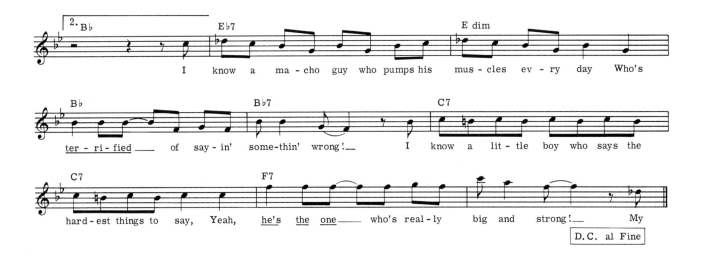

I know a ma-cho guy who pumps his mus-cles ev-ry day Who's ter-ri-fied ___ of say-in' some-thin' wrong! ___ I know a lit-tle boy who says the hard-est things to say, Yeah, he's the one ___ who's real-ly big and strong! ___ My

D.C. al Fine

The Stupid Song

Words and Music by Robin Batteau

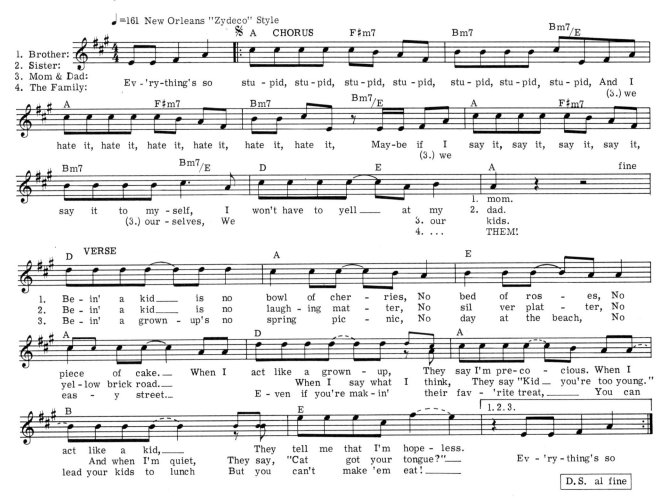

1. Brother:
2. Sister:
3. Mom & Dad:
4. The Family:

Ev-'ry-thing's so stu-pid, stu-pid, stu-pid, stu-pid, stu-pid, stu-pid, stu-pid, And I (3.) we hate it, hate it, hate it, hate it, hate it, hate it, May-be if I say it, say it, say it, say it, (3.) we say it to my-self, I won't have to yell ___ at my (3.) our-selves, We
1. mom.
2. dad.
3. our kids.
4. ... THEM!

VERSE

1. Be-in' a kid ___ is no bowl of cher-ries, No bed of ros-es, No
2. Be-in' a kid ___ is no laugh-ing mat-ter, No sil-ver plat-ter, No
3. Be-in' a grown-up's no spring pic-nic, No day at the beach, No

piece of cake. ___ When I act like a grown-up, They say I'm pre-co-cious. When I
yel-low brick road. ___ When I say what I think, They say "Kid ___ you're too young."
eas-y street. ___ E-ven if you're mak-in' their fav-'rite treat, ___ You can

act like a kid, ___ They tell me that I'm hope-less.
And when I'm quiet, They say, "Cat got your tongue?" ___
lead your kids to lunch But you can't make 'em eat! ___

Ev-'ry-thing's so

D.S. al fine

The Biggest Problem (Is in Other People's Minds)

Words and Music by Don Haynie

On My Pond

Words and Music by Kermit the Frog, with Sarah Durkee and Christopher Cerf

Something for Everyone

Words and Music by Carol Hall

The Turn of the Tide

Words and Music by Carly Simon and Jacob Brackman

Thank Someone

Music by Paul Jacobs, Words by Sarah Durkee

Afterword

I've often thought there ought to be a manual to hand to little kids, telling them what kind of planet they're on, why they don't fall off it, how much time they've probably got here, how to avoid poison ivy, and so on. I tried to write one once. It was called Welcome to Earth. But I got stuck on explaining why we don't fall off the planet. Gravity is just a word. It doesn't explain anything. If I could get past gravity, I'd tell them how we reproduce, how long we've been here, apparently, and a little bit about evolution. I didn't learn until I was in college about all the other cultures, and I should have learned that in the first grade. A first grader should understand that his or her culture isn't a rational invention; that there are thousands of other cultures and they all work pretty well; that all cultures function on faith rather than truth; that there are lots of alternatives to our own society. Cultural relativity is defensible and attractive. It's also a source of hope. It means we don't have to continue this way if we don't like it.

—*Kurt Vonnegut, Jr.*

Contributors

LYNN AHRENS has created and produced five Emmy-nominated children's television shows and, with fellow contributor and collaborator Stephen Flaherty, won the 1987 Richard Rodgers Award for their musical, *Lucky Stiff*.

BARBARA BASCOVE illustrated *Atalanta, Three Wishes*, and *Zachary's Divorce*.

ROBIN BATTEAU and fellow contributor David Buskin sing and perform together as the folk/pop duo, Buskin and Batteau.

ABRA BIGHAM is the coauthor of *Mary S*, a musical drama based on the life of Mary Shelley, which won Grand Prize in the New Works Competition sponsored by the 1987 American Musical Theatre Festival. She has also received a George London Award from the National Institue for Music Theatre and two National Penwomen's Association prizes.

GUY BILLOUT has written and illustrated children's books including his most recent work, *Journey*.

JUDY BLUME has written over forty books for children including *Are You There God, It's Me, Margaret; Then Again, Maybe I Won't; Tales of a Fourth Grade Nothing;* and *Otherwise Known as Sheila the Great*.

JACOB BRACKMAN is a former journalist (staff writer at *The New Yorker*, film critic for *Esquire* magazine) who has for some time worked in movies, theater and pop music. He collaborated with Carly Simon for nearly twenty years.

DONNA BROWN is an illustrator. Most recently, she illustrated *Virtual Reality Madness!* and *The History of Oklahoma*.

DAVID BUSKIN is a Clio-Award-winning jingle writer and a keyboard player who records and performs as half the folk/pop duo Buskin and Batteau. Mr. Buskin also wrote *Outdoor Games*.

ANN CAMERON wrote *The Stories Julian Tells*, an American Library Association Notable Book and a Parent's Choice Award winner. She is also a recipient of the Irma Simonton Black Award for contribution to children's literature.

CHRISTOPHER CERF was the founding editor-in-chief of *Sesame Street* Books, Records and Toys. He has written many songs for *Sesame Street* and its sister productions, *The Electric Company* and *Square One TV*, earning two Grammy Awards in the process. His book credits include *Kids: Day In and Day Out*, coedited with Elisabeth Scharlatt, which was nominated for an American Book Award. He is a former contributing editor of *National Lampoon*, and he conceived and coedited the best-selling newspaper parody *Not The New York Times*.

DAVID CHALK illustrated *Glad To Have a Friend Like You*.

EVE CHWAST specializes in woodcuts and three-dimensional papier-mache sculpture. She illustrated *Grandma's Latkes* by Malka Drucker and is Seymour Chwast's daughter.

SEYMOUR CHWAST is best known for designing and illustrating books, magazines, animated films, advertising, record covers, posters and packaging, and children's books. Mr. Chwast and his company Push Pin were honored at a two-month retrospective exhibition at the Louvre entitled "The Push Pin Style," and his work is in the permanent collections of New York's Museum of Modern Art, the Cooper-Hewitt Museum of the Smithsonian Institution and the Library of Congress. He was the 1985 American Institue of Graphic Arts Gold Medalist and is a member of the Art Director's Hall of Fame. His most recent books for children include *Mr. Merlin and the Turtle, Twelve Circus Rings*, and *The Alphabet Parade*.

LUCILLE CLIFTON is the author of the highly acclaimed Everett Anderson books as well as *Three Wishes* and *Lucky Stone*. She is a former Poet Laureat of Maryland and professor of literature at University of California at Santa Cruz.

TOM COOKE has been a mainstay of *Sesame Street* and Muppet publications. Mr. Cooke has won Merit Awards from the Society of Illustrators, The Design Institute of America and The Boston Art Director's Club.

CHRIS DEMAREST is a cartoonist and artist whose work has appeared in *Forbes, Redbook*, and *The Atlantic*. He has also written and illustrated several of his own children's books, including *No Peas for Nellie* and *All Aboard!*. He has illustrated over forty books for children.

LEO AND DIANE DILLON achieved the unprecedented honor of winning the Caldecott Medal in two consecutive years for *Why Mosquitoes Buzz in People's Ears* (1976) and *Ashanti to Zulu* (1977). Together, they have illustrated over thirty books.

SARAH DURKEE has written extensively for children's TV and theatre productions (*Sesame Street, The Muppets Show, Square One TV*).

JOHN PAUL ENDRESS illustrated *Boy Meets Girl, William's Doll,* and *It's All Right to Cry.*

THE FAT BOYS (Darren Robinson, Mark Morales and Damon Wimbley), an innovative rap group, are credited with inventing the human beat box. Their platinum album includes their hit single, "Jail House Rap." The group starred in two motion pictures, *Krush Groove* and *Disorderlies.*

STEPHEN FLAHERTY, with fellow contributor Lynn Ahrens, composed the score for *The Emperor's New Clothes* and contributed musical material to *When the Cookie Crumbles . . . .* In 1987, he and Ms. Ahrens won the Richard Rodgers Award for their musical *Lucky Stiff.*

JIMMY GLENN has collaborated with the Fat Boys on the lyrics to many of their songs, and served as a Project Consultant on their movie *Disorderlies.*

WHOOPI GOLDBERG, star of *Ghost, Sister Act* and *Sister Act II,* won a Golden Globe Award and an Oscar nomination for her performance in Steven Spielberg's *The Color Purple.* She also wrote and starred in her own one-woman Broadway show, directed by Mike Nichols.

BOBBY GOSH had a world-wide top ten hit by Dr. Hook and the Medicine Show, which earned Mr. Gosh two gold records. He has also recorded numerous albums of his own songs.

DAN GREENBERG has written many books including the children's book, *Jumbo the Boy and Arnold the Elephant.*

CAROL HALL received two Drama Desk Awards for the songs she wrote for the Tony-award winning *The Best Little Whorehouse in Texas.* Ms. Hall appeared in the Broadway production of *The Best Little Whorehouse in Texas* and starred in the Off-Broadway hit musical *I'm Getting My Act Together and Taking It on the Road.* She wrote the book, music and lyrics for the musical *To Whom It May Concern.* Her songs have been performed by such artists as Barbra Streisand, Harry Belafonte, Dolly Parton, Tony Bennett, Neil Diamond, and Big Bird.

SHELDON HARNICK has written the lyrics for many Broadway and Off-Broadway revues and musicals, including *Fiddler on the Roof, Fiorello, The Apple Tree,* and *The Rothschilds.*

BRUCE HART won an Emmy Award as one of the original writers for educational TV's *Sesame Street* series. He was also the lyricist for its title song. With Stephen Lawrence, he co-produced the musical portions of the soundtrack for *Free to Be . . . You and Me.*

DON HAYNIE, with his partner, vocalist and percussionist, Sheryl Samue, made the album *Life In the Circus.*

CARMINE INFANTINO played a pivotal role in the creation of *Superman* stories and art for more than thirty years. He came to DC Comics as a young artist in the 1950's and went on to become the Editorial Director and later Publisher of the company. He is credited with designing the "look" comic books have today.

PAUL JACOBS has a musical background that began with Julliard training and a Carnegie Hall piano debut at age nine. He was the composer and musical director of the long-running National Lampoon revue, *Lemmings,* and was at one time a keyboardist and producer for Meat Loaf. He has received two ASCAP theater awards and two Grammy nominations. The rock songs that he has written have earned him gold and platinum records.

SUSAN JEFFERS is a painter and graphic artist whose exquisite illustrations for such classics as *Cinderella, Hansel and Gretel, The Wild Swans* and *Black Beauty* have earned her international recognition. She won the Caldecott Honor in 1975 for *The Three Jovial Huntsmen,* and has received many prestigious awards and citations from such organizations as the Society of Illustrators, the International Reading Association, the Children's Book Council, the Child Study Association, and the American Institute of Graphic Arts. Ms. Jeffers has worked as a book designer in three major publishing firms and, in collaboration with the noted author-illustrator Rosemary Wells, founded a successful art and design studio.

JOYCE (GLASSMAN) JOHNSON most recently wrote the *Castle Land Curriculum: Especially for Four Year Olds.*

LONNI SUE JOHNSON, whose work has been seen in *The New Yorker, Gourmet* and many other national periodicals, is also the illustrator of the book, *57 Reasons Not to Have Nuclear War.* Her illustrations have been selected for special recognition by the Society of Illustrators.

MAVIS JUKES won a Newbery Honor for *Like Jake and Me,* and the Irma Simonton Black Award for *No One Is Going to Nashville.* She is also the author of *Blackberries in the Dark, Lights Around the Palm* and *Getting Even.*

KERMIT THE FROG was born in a swamp on the outskirts of Greensboro, Mississippi, and spent most of his early years training for a career in biological laboratory work. The lure of the entertainment world soon proved too strong to resist, however, and Kermit became an instant celebrity, with starring roles in Sesame Street, The Muppet Show and three Muppet motion pictures, and in the annual Macy's Thanksgiving Day parade with his very own balloon. Stardom hasn't spoiled him, however, and he is quick to share credit for his success with Muppet creator Jim Henson. "Every leap I've made," he says modestly, "Jim has had a hand in."

HILARY KNIGHT is best-known for his drawings in the children's (and adult) classic *Eloise,* written by Kay Thompson, which has been a best-seller for over thirty years. He has also been widely honored for the more than fifty other children's books he has illustrated, including *The Christmas Nutshell Library, The Twelve Days of Christmas* and Edward Lear's *The Owl and the Pussycat.*

ELAINE LARON, as a writer and lyricist for *The Electric Company,* wrote the lyrics for more than thirty of its songs.

STEPHEN LAWRENCE and fellow contributor Bruce Hart co-produced the musical portions of the soundtrack *Free to Be . . . You and Me.*

PIERRE LE-TAN is a novelist, humorist and illustrator whose work appears frequently in *The New Yorker* and *The New York Times Magazine*. Mr. Le-Tan, who sold his first cover illustration to *The New Yorker* when he was just seventeen years old, is the son of the noted Vietnamese artist Le Pho.

ARNIE LEVIN has been an award-winning designer, animator and cartoonist for over twenty years. He is best-known for the many covers and cartoons he has drawn for *The New Yorker*.

ARNOLD LOBEL is one of America's best-known and best-loved children's illustrators. His sensitive and delightful drawings appeared in more than seventy books, many of which he also wrote. Mr. Lobel won a Caldecott Honor for *Frog and Toad Are Friends*, a Newbery Honor for its sequel *Frog and Toad Together*, and a Caldecott medal for *Fables*.

PETRA MATHERS was chosen by *The New York Times* as one of the ten best children's illustrators of 1986. Her evocative artwork has earned her two Parents Choice Awards, for the book *Maria Theresa*, and for *Molly's New Washing Machine*. She was also a finalist for the 1986 Ezra Jack Keats Award.

JAMES McMULLAN has won numerous Gold and Silver Medals from the Society of Illustrators and was one of five artists whose work was featured in the "Masters of the Contemporary American Poster" exhibit in 1987 sponsored by the Lowell Gallery in New York City.

RICHARD McNEEL has earned an international reputation for his unique "three-dimensional" illustrations. Among the many publications which have featured his work are *Money, Working Mother, New Age,* and *Dun's Business Monthly.* Mr. McNeel is an associate of the Push Pin group.

BETTY MILES has written many books for children including *The Tortoise and the Hare, Sink or Swim,* and *I Would If I Could.*

SHELLEY MILLER has been working with Stephen Lawrence for several years. She plans to write more album material and musicals.

MIRIAM MINKOWITZ, a poet, philosopher, and high school teacher, has written children's stories for *Ms. Magazine.* She has a doctorate in Philosophy of Education.

JEFF MOSS wrote the music and lyrics for *The Muppets Take Manhattan*, for which he received an Academy Award nomination. His works for the stage include the musical *Double Feature,* and *In the Beginning.* Mr. Moss was one of the original creators of *Sesame Street.* While serving as head writer and composer-lyricist for the program, he won five Emmy Awards and wrote songs for four Grammy Award-winning records.

JOE ORLANDO is a cartoonist and illustrator whose work has been well-known over the years to readers of *Mad* magazine, *National Lampoon* and many other national periodicals.

JERRY PINKNEY has twice been the recipient of the Coretta Scott King Award and has also won the Christopher Award for "artistic excellence in affirming the human spirit." He has illustrated numerous children's books and has designed stamps for the U.S. Postal Service.

LETTY COTTIN POGREBIN is a founding editor of *Ms. Magazine* and a co-founder of the Free to Be Foundation and the Ms. Foundation. She is the author of several books, including *Growing Up Free, Family Politics* and *Getting Over, Getting Older,* and she also lectures nationally on children and family issues. She has won honors from such organizations as the National Council on Family Relations and the Family Service Association. Her work is featured in many textbooks and anthologies, among them *Marriage and Family, Beyond Sex Roles, Adolescent Life Experiences* and *Sexism and Youth.*

RALPH REESE is a veteran cartoonist and illustrator whose credits include *The National Lampoon,* several national advertising campaigns and drawings for children and adult books, ranging from the *Choose Your Own Adventure* series to *The Pentagon Catalog* by Henry Beard and Christopher Cerf.

CARL REINER won two Emmy Awards for his work on the Sid Caesar shows and six as producer and writer of the Dick Van Dyke series.

PHIL RESSNER is more than a famous actor, director, producer; he has also written several books for children including *August Explains, Jerome, At Night* and *The Park in the City.*

MARY RODGERS has written many classic children's books including *The Rotten Book, Freaky Friday,* and *A Billion for Boris.*

ARTIE RUIZ has designed and illustrated numerous books and their covers. Mr. Ruiz used his cousins as models for "Jimmy Says."

MARK SALTZMAN has written both songs and scripts for *Reading Rainbow, Sesame Street* and *Square One TV.* Among the stars who have performed his work are Patti Labelle, Wynton Marsalis and Itzhak Perlman. He won an Emmy Award in 1986 for his work on *Sesame Street.*

SHEL SILVERSTEIN has written and illustrated several best-selling children's classics, including *The Giving Tree, Where the Sidewalk Ends, A Light in the Attic,* and *Falling Up.* He is also a noted cartoonist, playwright, and songwriter. He has numerous hit songs, including *Sylvia's Mother* and *A Boy Named Sue.*

CARLY SIMON won a Grammy Award for being the best new recording artist of 1971 and another in 1972 for her hit song *You're So Vain.* Many of her songs have reached number one on the charts.

LINDA SITEA is both an artist and a writer. *Zachary's Divorce* is her first published story.

DEBRA SOLOMON is a cartoonist whose work has appeared in a wide variety of publications, from *Vogue* magazine to *The Anti-Apartheid Calendar*. She is also the illustrator of the book, *A Good Friend*, by Joseph Cohen.

GLORIA STEINEM is one of America's most widely read and critically acclaimed writers and editors. Two of her books, *Outrageous Acts and Everyday Rebellions* and *Marilyn: Norma Jeane*, have been best-sellers. Also internationally known as a feminist organizer and as a spokesperson on issues of equality, Ms. Steinem has appeared several times on the World Almanac's list of the 25 Most Influential Women in America. She is a co-founder of *Ms. Magazine*, the Free to Be Foundation, the Ms. Foundation for Women, and the National Women's Political Caucus and also helped start *New York* magazine, for whom she was a political columnist until 1972. She has been a recipient of the Front Page Award, the Clarion Award and the Ceres Medal from the United Nations.

JOHN STEPTOE is well-known for his groundbreaking picture books, including *Uptown*, *Train Ride* and *Birthday*. Published in 1969, *Stevie* was chosen as an American Library Association Notable Book and won the Society of Illustrators' Gold Medal in 1970. Mr. Steptoe has also won a Caldecott Honor for *The Story of Jumping Mouse*, and received The Boston Globe Horn Book Award for his 1987 book, *Mufaro's Beautiful Daughters*.

NORMAN STILES wrote for *The Merv Griffin Show*, *Fernwood Tonight*, *America Tonight* and *The Bad News Bears*. With Mel Brooks, Mr. Stiles co-created the television series *When Things Were Rotten*, and he has also authored several successful children's books. Since 1980, he has been head writer of *Sesame Street*.

SUSAN STILLMAN has taught illustration at the Parsons School of Design. Her work has been published in such periodicals as *The New York Times*, *New York* magazine, *Communications Arts*, and *Scholastic* as well as in several Society of Illustrators and Art Direction annuals.

PETER STONE has been President of the Dramatists Guild. His wide range of distinguished writing has won him an Academy Award (for *Father Goose*), and Emmy (for an episode of *The Defenders*), a Tony, a Drama Critics Circle Award and a Drama Desk Award (for *1776*), another Tony (for *Woman of the Year*) and a Mystery Writers of America Award (for *Charade*). With Carl Reiner, Mr. Stone was the coauthor of *Boy Meets Girl*, which Mel Brooks and Marlo Thomas performed on the *Free to Be . . . You and Me* soundtrack and television special.

SIMMS TABACK has received more than 100 awards from such organizations as the American Institute of Graphic Arts, the Art Directors Club of New York and the Society of Illustrators, and was included by *The New York Times* on their list of the best illustrators of children's books. Mr. Taback helped found both the Illustrators' Guild and the Graphic Artists Guild.

DOUG TAYLOR illustrated *Don't Dress Your Cat in an Apron*, *Housework*, and *My Dog Is a Plumber*.

MARLO THOMAS has won four Emmy Awards and the prestigious George Foster Peabody Broadcasting Award. As a member of two presidential commissions on women and children, she has created an alliance between the world of entertainment and social concern. She is a co-founder of the Free to Be Foundation as well as the Ms. Foundation.

JUDITH VIORST has written over twenty books of poetry and prose for both children and adults, and has been a contributing editor to *Redbook*. Among her best known books are *When Did I Stop Being Twenty and Other Injustices*, *How To Be Hip Over Thirty* and the national bestseller, *Necessary Losses*.

KURT VONNEGUT, JR. is the best-selling author of many novels, including *Slaughterhouse Five*, *Cat's Cradle*, *Player Piano*, *The Sirens of Titan* and *Blue Beard*. Mr. Vonnegut was inducted into the National Institute of Arts and Letters in 1970.

JANE WAGNER has received four Emmys for her work in television and a George Foster Peabody Award for her teleplay *I.T.* She also wrote the screenplay for *The Incredible Shrinking Woman*. She has received three Grammy nominations, and on Broadway she wrote and directed the Tony Award-winning *Appearing Nightly*. Most recently, she received the New York Drama Desk and New York Drama Critics Circle Awards for her work as writer-director of the play *The Search for Signs of Intelligent Life in the Universe*, starring Lily Tomlin, which has also been a best-selling book.

GARY ZAMCHICK is well known for his witty cartoons as well as his elaborate computer graphics. His work appeared weekly in the Arts & Leisure section of *The New York Times*. Mr. Zamchick worked at Push Pin Studios and also spent two years at Time, Inc. designing children's educational software. He is president of his own graphics firm DadaBase Design.

CHARLOTTE ZOLOTOW is the author of over seventy books for children. Among her most cherished books are *William's Doll*, *Mr. Rabbit and the Lovely Present*, and *My Grandson Lew*. Ms. Zolotow is the recipient of numerous awards including the prestigious Kerlan Award (1986) for her body of work and her contribution to children's literature.